The
Well-Armored
Child

A Parent's Guide to Preventing Sexual Abuse

Joelle Casteix

RIVER GROVE
BOOKS

Published by River Grove Books
Austin, TX
www.rivergrovebooks.com

Distributed by River Grove Books

For ordering information or special discounts for bulk purchases, please contact River Grove Books at PO Box 91869, Austin, TX 78709, 512.891.6100.

Design and composition by Greenleaf Book Group
Cover design by Greenleaf Book Group

Publisher's Cataloging-in-Publication Data is available.

ISBN: 978-1-63299-039-6

First Edition

Other Edition(s):
eBook ISBN: 978-1-63299-040-2

For Mike

"Shame derives its power from being unspeakable."

—Brené Brown

Contents

If You Need Help . . .

Before we begin, let's focus on one crucial action you can take right now (or at any time) to help anyone who may be suffering from sexual abuse: *Report it.* If you encounter any of the following situations, get help immediately:

- Someone tells you they have been raped.

- You have seen or suspect abuse.

- You or someone you know is suicidal.

- You have come across anything that you suspect is child pornography.

In any of these situations, do not second-guess yourself or make the mistake of reporting to your church, school, youth group, or other organization. Institutions like these are not in the sex abuse investigation business. They are not trained in criminal investigations.

Moreover, they have shown time and time again that, in most cases, they will protect their reputation over kids.

Instead, go to the police. If you are scared to go alone, take a trusted friend with you.

If you suspect abuse, call the Childhelp National Child Abuse Hotline at 800-4-A-CHILD. The hotline's crisis counselors can walk you through the process of reporting and help you talk through what you have seen or suspect.

If you are suicidal, or if you know someone who is, call the National Suicide Prevention Lifeline at 800-273-TALK (8255).

Don't wait until it's too late.

Foreword

I didn't have to be a statistic.

As a teenager, I was sexually abused by one of my teachers. By the time the abuse ended, I was pregnant and had contracted a sexually transmitted disease. Other teachers and administrators knew I was being sexually molested, but instead of doing the right thing and calling the police, they remained quiet. My abuser got off easy. His victims were given a life sentence.

My abuse didn't have to happen. It could have been stopped at the first signs of abuse—or prevented altogether. My life didn't have to take this course. Had adults recognized the "red flags," done the right thing, and reported it to the police, I could have been helped, and other victims could have been spared.

As I moved out of childhood and became an adult, I came to terms with my abuse and how it was covered up. I realized that in order to heal, I needed to make an immediate difference. So I dedicated my career to helping other victims of abuse and raising awareness about the larger issues of abuse prevention. I started out as a volunteer, just telling my story. Soon, I had become a professional.

These days, I have an extraordinary and immensely rewarding job: I expose child sex offenders and the cover-up of child sex abuse. I also educate communities on the larger issues surrounding child sex crimes. I have traveled the world and been on the TV news in every major city in the United States. I host a successful blog, Casteix.com and have worked with thousands of child sex abuse victims in the United States and abroad. I uncover information about abusers and learn their patterns so I can reach out to more victims who are suffering alone in silence.

You would think this kind of job—catching bad guys, rescuing children—would make for rousing cocktail party conversations. But during the past ten years of doing this work, people seldom, if ever, have asked me more about the abuse and cover-up I have helped expose. They don't ask me about the scandals within large religious or institutional organizations. Instead, I get the same passionate question over and over again: *What can I do to make sure my child does not become a victim?*

The abuse prevention movement has neglected our most important audience: parents. We've done studies and trained therapists and changed public perception, but we've never created an easy-to-read book for parents—a "tool kit" for *preventing* child sexual abuse. Parenting books cover almost every topic under the sun. After my own child was born, I was deluged with tomes that covered everything from feeding to bullying to rashes to choosing a preschool. One book, however, was noticeably absent. It was the book that could have changed the course of my life as a child. And here it is now, in your hands: the book that can help parents take action to prevent their child from becoming another victim.

This information is important, and it is priceless. Parents will do anything to help armor their child against sexual abuse. But guess what:

Raising a well-armored, protected child is easy. It does not involve discussions about sex. And it can help empower any child about their bodies for the rest of their lives. Who doesn't want that for their son or daughter?

I am a victim with a powerful and relevant story to tell. I am a parent. I have worked with more than a thousand victims of child sexual abuse and read the depositions of hundreds of predators. I now work closely with advocates, educators, and leaders in the field of child sexual abuse treatment. I've presented strategies on child sex abuse exposure and prevention in front of thousands of people across the country. I've been in the trenches, and I am using knowledge to help parents stop the cycle of abuse. Academics and therapists have written wonderful books about the effects and aftereffects of abuse, but when it comes to prevention and awareness, a survivor advocate is the best, most knowledgeable person to tell the story.

This is a book that could not have been written twenty years ago. I hope that, in twenty years, more and more communities won't need such a book. For now, though, it's information you need—and you can handle it. The scariest things in life can also be the most difficult things to discuss. This is especially true when it comes to child sexual abuse. But keep reading, because you will learn that preventing abuse is much easier than you think.

Introduction

Why You Need This Book

Child sexual abuse happens everywhere. It happens in homes, schools, churches, youth organizations, camps, neighborhoods, community centers, and public facilities. The statistics are pretty vague; this is a horribly underreported crime. There are no accurate statistics about how many children are sexually abused each year. Conventional wisdom says that one in six boys and one in four girls in this country will be victims of sexual abuse before the age of eighteen, but it is virtually impossible to find a source for these numbers. According to the US Department of Justice, approximately one in six children will be the victim of sexual violence by the time they reach eighteen.[1] Another study, by the Crimes Against Children Research Center, says that one in five girls and one in twenty boys is a victim of abuse.[2] Any way you look at it, that's pretty grim news.

But your child does not have to be a statistic. With the information in this book, you can raise a well-armored child who is safer from abuse.

You Don't Want to Raise an "Easy Target"

Unfortunately, there is no "vaccine" that can guarantee your child will be 100 percent safe from sexual abuse. No magic bullet exists that will protect your child from predators. But there are a few simple things that may lower the chances of your child being abused by 95 percent. *That's what this book will help you accomplish.* Nothing will make your child "abuse proof," but *armoring* your child against abuse is the best gift you can give him or her. And taking these crucial steps toward prevention is much easier and far less painful than you imagine.

This book offers tools that exist nowhere else, and with their help, you can keep your child from becoming a statistic. You can raise a child who is empowered about his or her body. You can raise a child who feels comfortable talking to you. You can give your child concrete body boundaries so he or she has few doubts about whether something bad is happening. Not only that, but you can give your child the tools to help other children. Children who are protected and know their own boundaries are more likely to see when those boundaries are violated with other children and more likely to tell their parents about what they see. When more children recognize when things are wrong and report what they see, more child sex predators are stopped. Children who understand and respect their boundaries are also more likely to report schoolyard violence and bullying, because there is no misunderstanding about what is right and wrong when it comes to other people's bodies.

No one wants to raise a child who is vulnerable, because that child attracts abuse. A vulnerable child is one who yearns for adult attention, no matter the form that attention takes. The vulnerable child can come from a broken home or from an intact home where adults are dealing with addiction issues, family tragedy, or mental illness. Whatever the issues, the parents will not or cannot give the child the help and proper attention that he or she needs. Sometimes the vulnerable child has physical, emotional, social, or cognitive disabilities that are not addressed or properly treated. At other times, the vulnerable child is dealing with issues of his or her own sexuality. Or perhaps the vulnerable child is a victim of childhood trauma that adversely affected brain development. Whatever his or her background, this vulnerable child becomes an "easy target"—like a bank safe that has been left unlocked, so to speak—allowing the molester easy and quick access. Unfortunately, many parents—*through no fault of their own*—have no idea how vulnerable their child is until it's too late.

You Need an Expert Who Has Been "In the Trenches"

Most books about child health and safety issues are written by people with lots of letters after their names, and rightfully so. Doctors, scientists, researchers, and legal experts usually know the most about their respective fields. Most of the time, they are the go-to people for accurate information on almost any topic under the sun. But child sexual abuse is different.

Who am I? I am not a doctor or a researcher. But I am an expert. I have spoken with more than a thousand adult victims of child sexual abuse, getting into the deepest details about how, why, and when their abuse occurred. I know who the perpetrators are and how they got such easy access to their victims. I have met with victims in Delaware and California, in the territory of Guam and in remote Eskimo villages in western Alaska, and in almost every region in between. They have trusted me enough to reveal their stories, show me their court documents, share photos and letters, tell the horrific details, and help me figure out patterns of abuse and cover-up. They trusted me when they would trust no one else.

Why? Because I am one of them. I am an adult victim of child sexual abuse.

From the ages of fifteen to seventeen, I was sexually abused by one of my high school teachers at a Catholic high school in Orange County, California. Throughout the entirety of the abuse, other teachers and administrators at the school knew I was being sexually molested and did *nothing* to help me. They did not report the crime. They did not warn other kids. Instead they protected the man who raped me (and other girls) and wrote him a glowing letter of recommendation when he quietly resigned from his teaching job. He got off easy. His victims were given a life sentence.

By the time I was finally healed enough to do something, I had no rights in the criminal courts. I could not help police put my abuser behind bars. But in 2002, California passed a special law allowing adult victims of child sexual abuse to file lawsuits in civil courts between January 1 and December 31, 2003, no matter when the abuse occurred. I came forward and filed a civil lawsuit at the age of thirty-two. After more than two years of litigation, I was granted access to more than two hundred pages of secret personnel documents about my abuse and how the school and the Roman Catholic Diocese of Orange, California, covered it up. *They knew.* And instead of calling the police or getting me help, they allowed my abuser to move out of state and avoid criminal prosecution.

On one hand, these documents made me feel vindicated. Many people could not comprehend that I had been sexually abused at such a prestigious high school and that the people in charge had covered it up. No one wanted to believe that something so horrible was true. But the documents proved I had been right all along. On the other hand, I felt utterly betrayed. How could teachers and school administrators—adults who were responsible for my safety—have allowed me to be abused? Why didn't anyone stop it? Why wasn't anyone punished? Was I responsible in some way?

Getting validation in the court system and access to secret evidence about the cover-up was an essential step on my road to healing. Other victims, I knew, needed to learn the truth about their abuse as I had.

Abusers needed to be held accountable. Victims needed power and responsibility in order to heal. Even more, the men and women who covered up for abusers needed to be exposed.

As a result, I turned my passion into my job: I expose child sex offenders and the cover-up of child sex abuse all over the country. I do research on abusers, get the media to cover the stories, and act as a national spokesperson for victims when the big stories hit the news. When victims come forward for the first time, often I am the person they call. I work with large and small nonprofits to spread the word about prevention and to help victims use the legal system to get justice. I also educate communities on the larger issues surrounding child sex crimes.

I have listened to victims and learned and studied their painful path before, during, and after abuse. I have seen the telltale patterns of child predators and their abuse. Every story is important, and every case is unique. Still, during the past decade (and even in my own case) I have seen the same issues over and over again. Problems that could have been an "easy fix" for some families went unnoticed, leaving a child vulnerable to sexual abuse. It could have been something as simple as how a parent reacts to a child who misbehaves, or as easy as teaching a child the proper names of his or her body parts. Small changes could have made the difference between a safe child and a vulnerable child. Small changes could have saved me and countless others.

So now, I teach parents about the small changes they can make to keep their children safe.

Many wonderful books have been written about abuse. Victims have bravely put pen to paper to write memoirs of hurt, loss, and betrayal. Academics have done wonderful studies on the effects and aftereffects of abuse. Therapists have created useful books and tools to help victims through the healing process. But this book goes where none of these have: It reveals a parent's role in prevention.

This book is the culmination of more than a thousand case studies of abuse, including my firsthand experience. It also taps the passion of every adult victim of abuse—the hope of ensuring that today's children are protected against abuse, so the horrible crimes that happened to me and others will not be repeated.

You Need to Hear the Good News

Let's start with good news: Our children are much safer than they were when I was a child in the 1970s and '80s. Why?

We Are More Informed about Abuse

As a society, we are far more informed about abuse. We talk about abuse in polite conversations and discuss the subject openly in many of our homes and schools. The Catholic clergy and Boy Scout sex abuse scandals of the 1990s and 2000s have started national and international discussions. Child sex crimes are no longer something we ignore or are too embarrassed to discuss.

We No Longer Blame the Victim

In more and more cases, our society is beginning to stop blaming the victim. When I was a kid (I was born in 1970), no one talked about sexual abuse. In fact, child sex abuse was not only repugnant, but it was seen as shameful and embarrassing. It was never discussed. The victim brought the stigma of shame to his or her family, and the abuse became a "dirty little secret." By the 1980s when I was abused, little had changed. My parents and school blamed *me* for being molested by my high school choir director. It wasn't because my parents were malicious child-haters. It was because they did not understand the dynamic of child sexual abuse and how a child is groomed into becoming a victim. They expected me to have adult sensibilities. They thought abuse was uncommon. They truly believed that my behavior invited my abuser to sexually molest me and showed that I wanted it. What had happened to me (to them, it was a matter of *what I had done*) was shameful and reflected badly on them.

My parents were products of their generation, which was also a generation plagued with abuse. Child victims who had been my parents' peers were ashamed and isolated; they stayed silent, part of a vicious cycle. This sense of shame was a perspective that was handed down both subliminally and obviously over the years. People can be very mean to sex abuse victims, especially in religious groups. The administrators at my high school, however, were even more malicious in their actions. Doing things like blaming victims for abuse, covering up evidence, and supporting abusers were concerted efforts on their part to protect the criminal and the school. Fortunately, these kinds of reactions are no longer the norm. The simple fact that you're reading this book shows how far we have come.

This leads me to the next bit of good news . . .

We No Longer Live in Denial

Some people seem to think that because *they* were not abused, *no one* was abused—and since no one talked about abuse, this skewed logic is understandable. My dearly departed mother-in-law used to tell me that when she was a child in the 1930s and '40s, there was no such thing as child sexual abuse. In Lincoln, Nebraska, where she grew up, she said, everyone was happy and the children played freely without fear.

I beg to differ. The children may have played freely and the adults may have been without fear, but child sexual abuse was there. I can promise you that. In every city in every state of the union, there were cases of child sexual abuse—then and now. The victims, without the awareness, support, and defense of their communities, were relegated to lives of fear, shame, and silence. In many cases, young children didn't even have the language capabilities or the vocabulary to describe what had happened to them; the terms we hear today simply weren't used. There were many victims of abuse in Lincoln. They just never said anything.

My grandmother was a little more forthcoming. She told me that when she was a child in the early 1920s, she would watch her mother chase away her mentally ill grandfather with a broom to keep him from, as she put it, "raping the little girls." And sadly, if he caught and abused one of the little girls, the child was cleaned up and then punished for letting the old man get to her. Escape was seldom an option. In fact, I have worked with victims who enlisted in World War II because enlisting early and going to war was the *only* option to get away from an abuser.

Victims today have much better options for reporting abuse, getting support, and healing. Police know how to interview very young victims in a safe way. The courts understand that all children—even teens—are scared to report and testify. Many parents know that child abuse is a crime, not something that their child "asked for." The public and the courts are giving victims a chance at justice. And while no one ever wants to come forward and admit that he or she has been sexually abused, our society is getting better at encouraging victims to come out of the shadows of shame and silence.

We Can Turn to Law Enforcement

Another reason things are better: The police are engaged in punishing predators. In the past, if victims did report, cops rarely investigated the crimes. Why? In many cases, no one believed the victim. In other cases, parents wrongly feared that the legal process would further traumatize the child or bring shame on the family. In the worst cases, the predator was an important community member, so police and prosecutors knew they could never get a conviction. Fortunately, for the most part, those days are over, and our police stations and prosecutor offices are staffed with well-trained, passionate, and compassionate men and women who are dedicated to stopping abuse. Today, police action is one of the best crime deterrents we have.

Abuse Is Not as Common as You Think

There is even more good news: Child sex abuse happens much less frequently than television and other media would lead you to believe. The twenty-four-hour news cycle must continually produce "breaking stories" that bring in ratings and revenue. What brings in top ratings? Fear. As a result, the news media will cover child abduction, abuse, murder, and sex abuse stories ad nauseam because those topics are emotionally charged, tap our biggest fears, and bring in the highest ratings.

I used to be a print journalist, so I understand the system: If it bleeds, it leads. News organizations want more hits on their websites and more subscriptions. Television stations want higher ratings. The best way to accomplish this is to create "sensational" stories that draw people in and keep them glued to the set or screen. The most shocking stories—the ones we cannot turn away from—usually include horrible things happening to children. We know many of these kidnapped and sexually abused children by name and have followed their stories for decades: Elizabeth Smart, Jaycee Dugard, and Polly Klaas (who was murdered). We are pulled into their stories because it is human nature. We believe that by watching and learning, we could prevent the same thing from happening to the children in our lives.

I am not here to wag my finger at the news media. They perform a valuable service and have been many victims' best friend and ally when it comes to exposing abuse. If it weren't for brave members of the media believing victims' stories of abuse, thousands of predators across the United States would have never been exposed. The media has done what many institutions could not: root out abusers, expose crimes, and shame people who cover up abuse. But this constant coverage can be overwhelming and misleading. All too often, parents take it as firm evidence that abuse is on the rise in their own neighborhood.

So turn off the TV once in a while and realize that your child is far safer now than he or she might have been twenty, thirty, or forty years ago. This book will show you why.

We No Longer Stand for Bullying

That's right, there is even good news about bullying. Reading the stories on the Internet today, you might think we are a nation scourged with bullies: hordes of mean-spirited alpha dogs who use power and intimidation to make the lives of the other half of the world miserable. But as a society, we now recognize and better understand bullying, both online and offline. We know that victims of bullying are vulnerable to adult manipulation. We know that victims who already suffer from depression are more likely to engage in self-destructive behaviors, even suicide. We are no longer a culture that tells our kids to "suck it up and take it like a man." Opening the discussion about bullying has made kids more likely to tell their parents if they experience or witness it. And early intervention in bullying can help prevent child sexual abuse.

Why? A bullied child is a perfect target for a predator, because that child yearns for adult protection, attention, and love. So because we are now able to identify and stop bullying sooner, we can help save kids before they become targets.

You Need to Face the Not-So-Good News

Unfortunately, alongside the strides we have made in preventing child sex abuse, there's plenty of information that is not so encouraging. The reality is frightening, to say the least.

Abuse Affects Everyone

The bad news is, as your child grows up, chances are that he or she will know someone who has been sexually abused as a child. It could be a best friend, a boyfriend or girlfriend, a spouse, a younger person who looks up to your child, or an acquaintance. No matter how much you try to shield your child from the effects of child sexual abuse, he or she will be affected. Growing up, even if your child is not a victim herself, he or she will need to understand how to empathize with a victim, how to spot abuse, and how to report it or reach out for help.

Being the partner or friend of a victim of abuse can be traumatic, but this trauma is made worse when the supporter does not understand abuse, abuse patterns, and grooming, and does not have a support system of his or her own for help and guidance. As your child grows older, and as it becomes age appropriate to learn more about the dynamics of sexual abuse, you can help him or her understand the crime and its effects on victims and their loved ones. This book will show you how.

Abuse Can Happen Anywhere

Here's more bad news: Abuse can and does happen everywhere. I have worked with incest victims and with victims of nuns, priests, coaches, teachers, neighbors, family friends, and Boy Scout troop leaders from all over the country. Predators lurk and thrive in places where they can easily find vulnerable children.

What's more, we no longer live with the fallacy that a child is safe if his or her teachers and coaches are all women. While it's true there are far fewer female child predators than male child predators, high-profile cases have opened our eyes to the real and significant threat that women abusers pose. Many cases of abuse by women are not reported and investigated, mostly due to stereotypes and the age-old "rite of passage" archetype. But boys and girls who are sexually abused by women suffer the same wounds that other victims endure. The damage is just as great.

This reality leads to a knee-jerk defense used by such organizations as the Catholic Church and the Boy Scouts: *Abuse happens everywhere. So why is everyone picking on us?* They are right on the first count. But the reason there has been so much attention on the scandal in big organizations is because of the concerted cover-up of abuse and abusers. Where there is cover-up and secrecy, abuse thrives. Had church or Scout leaders done the right thing when they discovered that a priest or volunteer was abusing kids (i.e., called the cops), the abuse and the scandal would have been far less widespread.

Not all churches are bad, and not all priests are child sex offenders. But as former US President Ronald Reagan once said about relations with the Soviet Union, "Trust, but verify." It's okay to go to church and attend Scout meetings; it is also okay to demand criminal histories of everyone who comes in contact with your child, and it is more than okay for you to hold organizational leaders (especially those in churches) to the highest standards possible. This book will discuss in depth the failures of some of our most trusted institutions and how you can armor your child against abuse *at any age* from *any predator*.

Predators Are Smart

The sad truth is, the majority of predators are never caught. Child sexual abuse remains a vastly underreported crime. What's more, due to criminal and civil statutes of limitation (SOLs), by the time the victim is finally whole and healed enough to report, often it is far too late for law enforcement to do anything.

A statute of limitation is a fancy legal term for the maximum amount of time a victim has to come forward in the criminal or civil justice systems to prosecute a crime. In some states, the SOL is only two or three years after a child turns eighteen. Many victims of child sex crimes are still in the depths of despair over their abuse when they are in their twenties and thirties. Other victims, because of the power of the predator and the victim's own immaturity, don't even understand that what happened to them was a crime. Still other victims blame themselves or descend into addiction or anger issues out of self-loathing, and they don't recover enough to seek justice or report the abuse until it's too late—if they recover at all.

Predators know this. They abuse children for the very reason that children can be easily manipulated into compliance. They know their crime will never be reported, because their victims are too scared, too hurt, or too indoctrinated to go to the cops in time.

Child predators are cunning, charismatic, talented, smart, and funny. They tend to surround themselves with friends and a strong community to have greater access to kids. They carefully groom, indoctrinate, and "sucker" adults, not just children. They ensure that if a child comes forward, adults will rally around the predator ("He has been to my house. He would *never* hurt a child!"). I have seen churches hire and support *convicted* child molesters, saying, "The cops got it all wrong" or "The sex was really consensual." Find this hard to believe? It happens far more often than you think.

When a child predator is arrested and convicted, there is no guarantee that he or she will stop abusing. A case in point is Mary Kay Letourneau, an elementary school teacher who was arrested and convicted of molesting sixth-grade student Vili Fualaau in 1997. Two weeks after being released from serving a six-month sentence for second-degree child rape (and after giving birth to her victim's child), Letourneau was found in a car, molesting the now fourteen-year-old Fualaau. She was sent back to jail, where she gave birth to her second child by the boy. Like Letourneau, some predators are repeatedly arrested, while others slowly assimilate back into society without completely disclosing their past. The vast majority are never arrested at all, much less convicted.

This book will show you how smart predators groom children and why they often go free. It will also reveal how you can help your child report crimes, and how you can help lawmakers create victim-friendly laws that can put predators behind bars.

The Shame Can Be Devastating

Religion is a double-edged sword. Unfortunately, although faith can be a path to healing and wholeness for many victims, in many cases it plays a role in further wounding the victim. Depending on the religious tone of the community, victims can be plagued with implied "moral faults" because they are no longer innocent in the ways of sex. Especially for young men or women who made a public vow of chastity until marriage, the abuse is not only criminal but a broken promise to God. This can be utterly devastating. For many victims dealing with this kind of shame, suicide can seem like a viable option. For victims—of either sex—who believe they are worthless, broken, and dirty in the eyes of God, the depths of despair are vast and sometimes inescapable.

This book will show you how to help a victim realize that "purity" is not an issue when it comes to child sexual abuse. A victim of child sexual abuse is as beautiful and "pure" in the eyes of God as a child who has never been abused.

An Abused Child May Someday Disclose to Your Child

Many victims of child sexual abuse do come forward, in some way, while they are still children. They will confide in a trusted friend who usually swears to keep the "secret." That friend, many times, is also a child. Lacking a trusting relationship with an adult who understands abuse and how to report it, the child confidant keeps the secret and thus shares the burden of abuse. Even worse, the child who is trusted with the secret is forced into adult situations and adult decisions—without an adult to help.

Don't force your child to make adult decisions before he or she is ready. By reading this book and taking action, you will empower your child not only to repel abusers, but also to react appropriately when a friend comes forward as a victim of abuse.

Child Sexual Abuse Is a Huge Burden on Our Society

This sad reality cannot be overstated. The list of adverse aftereffects of child sexual abuse is daunting. Victims can suffer from mental health issues such as depression, psychosis, and suicidal thoughts. They endure self-destructive behaviors like cutting, addiction, and anger. They have difficulty integrating into society and agonize over sexuality issues. They often are unable to form lasting relationships or fall prey to domestic abuse. They might even engage in criminal behavior. When you add up the costs to our communities—for mental health care, police services, jails, adoption and foster care, victim services, drug and alcohol rehab, food stamps, welfare, and other social services that many victims and their families require—the price tag is staggering. Through all these avenues, we can help adult victims of child sexual abuse after the fact so they can heal, become more whole, and function as productive members of society. But the only way to reduce the burden on our families, our communities, and our nation is to make sure the abuse does not happen in the first place.

To do that, you must educate your child about his or her body and how to stay safe—and doing so is much easier and less painful than you may think.

5 Common Misconceptions about Child Sex Abuse Education

If you want to equip your child to fend off sexual predators, education is the answer. When you raise a well-armored child—a child who immediately knows that certain things are wrong and trusts you enough to tell you what's going on—predators can sense it, and they are more likely to leave your child alone.

But as a parent, you probably harbor concerns about educating your child in a way that is appropriate. Misconceptions about sex abuse education may leave you hesitant to take what are actually quite simple, realistic steps toward protecting your child at any age. So let's debunk some of these misconceptions.

Misconception #1: "My child is too young to know about sex."

Parents, understandably, don't want their children to be too "worldly" too soon. But armoring your child against sex abuse does not have to include talking about sex. You can empower your child with all the necessary tools *without* destroying his or her innocence. A toddler or young child who knows the proper name of his or her body parts is already empowered. You do not need to get into further uncomfortable discussions about biology, where babies come from, sexuality, shame, morality, or religious views on sex.

Misconception #2: "Children shouldn't be exposed to discussions about sexual abuse."

Talking about sexual abuse is not an appropriate discussion for young children, and in fact it makes many people uncomfortable even when among adults. But you do not have to talk about abuse in order to teach your child to be safer from predators. Instead you are simply teaching him or her to be safe, to communicate, and to have strong boundaries.

By the time a child enters high school, chances are that your child has already been exposed to the reality of sexual abuse. Perhaps your teen has heard rumors about abuse, a friend has disclosed his or her abuse, or your teen has witnessed or suspected an abusive relationship. This book will give you the tools to encourage your child to come to you with any questions about or suspicions of abuse—and to trust you enough to tell you if something happens to him or her.

Misconception #3: "The real problem isn't ongoing abuse—it's 'stranger danger.'"

Teaching your child to avoid strangers is not enough to prevent abuse. You may be telling yourself that you know what a predator looks like, but we are not talking about the guy in the trench coat hanging out in the corner of the schoolyard. Predators are cunning, and they come in all shapes and sizes. Yes, there is a danger of your child being the victim of a stereotypical kidnapping, but according to data from the US Department of Justice, your child is more likely to be bitten by a shark or struck by lightning.[3]

In fact, the vast majority of child sexual abuse is perpetrated by someone the child loves and trusts—someone *you* love and trust. Of course you must teach your child common sense about stranger danger and being safe in public. But telling your kid that if anyone touches him, you will go and kill the guy is not enough. It might even prevent your child from telling you about abuse, because no child wants to see his parents kill someone and go to jail.

Empowering your child with knowledge will make him or her a "hard target." A well-equipped child who is educated about boundaries and his or her body is the best defense against not just the guy in the trench coat but the other 99 percent of child predators.

Misconception #4: "My child already knows how to avoid those situations."

Think your child doesn't need sex abuse education or is too smart to fall prey to a sexual predator? Some of the smartest and savviest people I know were sexually abused as children. Predators are smart, and they are experts at earning kids' trust, fear, and love. And many of them are protected by institutions that you trust implicitly—whether they are religious, secular, or community based. Let's face it: Your child is no match against a predator *and* the Catholic or Mormon church, or the Boy Scouts of America, or a local community sports organization.

Furthermore, you might be surprised to learn about the abusive situations children face beyond just the archetypal "pervert." Women teachers, for example, pose a significant risk, particularly because of a lack of reporting and age-old attitudes such as "Boys can't be raped by women." In many cases, because of the manipulative nature of grooming, the child actually loves the abuser. More than one predator has not been reported because the child victim feared what his parents would do to the abuser when they found out.

Misconception #5: "My school/church gave me a book about child sex abuse and what to do."

If your school or church has a lawyer, that book about sex abuse was written for the sole purpose of protecting your school or church from civil or criminal liability. I know that sounds harsh, but it's the reality. It doesn't mean that you shouldn't trust your school or that your church is staffed by bad people who hire child sex abusers. It means that their first priority in writing the book is the *institution*, not *your child*.

Likewise, you may feel sure that your school, church, or club "safe environment" program is working. But consider the case of convicted child sex offender Mark Gurries, who in 2012 was allowed to work at a Catholic parish festival with children in San Jose, California. When the pastor was asked why, he told angry parents that they must be good Christians and "forgive" Gurries. The kicker: Every staff member and volunteer at the parish was required to undergo fingerprinting and a "safe environment" program.

Safety programs can give parents a false sense of security. They teach parents, most of whom would never hurt a child, how to properly behave in certain situations. But I have never heard of a predator who said, "Gosh, this program changed my life. I am never going to prey on another child." Safe environment programs teach good parents how not to abuse kids. They don't teach parents how to keep predators away from their children.

That's what this book will teach you.

* * *

Fortunately, your child is probably safer than you think—but that shouldn't stop you from educating yourself and taking precautions to prevent him or her from becoming vulnerable to predators, sexual abuse, and cover-up. Arming your child with the "no secrets" rule and other information and attitudes can save him or her from abuse. No matter the age, you can help your child learn about abuse in an appropriate way, identify abuse and predatory behaviors, and report abusive crimes.

This book will show you how.

Part One

The Basics

Chapter 1

What Is Child Sexual Abuse? Myths, Signs, and Healthy Behaviors

Child sex abuse is a devastating crime that affects approximately one in six children in the United States before age eighteen. But what exactly is meant by the term *child sex abuse*? And how can parents recognize the warning signs before it's too late?

What Is Child Sex Abuse?

The federal government defines child sex abuse as follows, according to the Child Abuse Prevention and Treatment Act:

> The employment, use, persuasion, inducement, entice-
> ment, or coercion of any child to engage in, or assist any
> other person to engage in, any sexually explicit conduct or
> simulation of such conduct for the purpose of producing
> a visual depiction of such conduct; or [t]he rape, and in
> cases of caretaker or interfamilial relationships, statutory

rape, molestation, prostitution, or other form of sexual exploitation of children, or incest with children.

That's a complicated definition, but it covers a lot of ground. Fortunately, the law acknowledges that children do not have the mental capabilities of adults and includes the fact that children are not only physically forced into abuse, but can be *persuaded, enticed, or induced*—a factor in grooming, which is discussed at length in chapter 4.

The definition includes sexually explicit conduct—which means that children who are rubbed, touched, kissed sexually over or under their clothes, penetrated, or forced to perform oral sex or other activities are also victims of abuse. It also includes children who are forced to engage in sexual conduct with other children for the pleasure of adults, and children who are sexually abused by other children.

Furthermore, the definition includes child pornography (also known as "child abuse images"), child sex trafficking, incest, and *statutory rape*, a legal term that has been used to scapegoat teen sex-abuse victims.

No one wants to think that these kinds of things can happen to their children. But they can, and they do. Despite the official definition, child sex abuse has nothing to do with sex. It is a crime of power. The purpose of this book is to give you the tools that will help empower your child to avoid the risk as much as possible. And unless you know what sexual abuse is, you can't prevent it.

It's important to realize that the faces of child sexual abuse are as varied as the victims. A child who is French-kissed and photographed naked by her uncle is a victim, as is the child who is forced into the sex trade at age fourteen. The young boy who is sodomized by his parish priest is horribly damaged, as is the teen girl who is molested by her high school teacher. And because a child's brain is still forming throughout all this abuse, no one knows exactly how damaging any of these acts might be.

My point is this: It is not our place to judge victims, minimize their abuse, or blame them for making mistakes that may have contributed to falling into the hands of a predator. When we minimize the abuse of a class of victims, whether they are trafficked children, homosexual boys, or teenage victims of incest, we give predators a break and silence crime victims.

The one area this book is not going to discuss is sexual relationships between teens on the margins of age eighteen—such as a nineteen-year-old boy having a sexual relationship with a seventeen-year-old girl. Instead we will focus on adults in positions of power: parents, relatives, teachers, coaches, community leaders, clerics, or any adult who can make decisions about the child and his or her welfare. If an adult can destroy a child's reputation, the adult is in a position of power. If the adult is in the position to physically, mentally, or emotionally hurt the child or other people, that adult is in a position of power. And an adult who uses that power to manipulate, entice, or coerce children and teens into sexual actions is exercising criminal behavior.

Other than that, no type of sexual abuse is a "gray area." When a teacher, family member, or other supposedly trustworthy adult engages in any kind of sexual activity with a child or young student, that is criminal. Some may say that teenage girls and boys "should know better," but the sexual abuse of teenagers by adults in positions of power is damaging, isolating, and most important, a crime. For me as a teenager, the abuse was devastating. It destroyed my family and most of my relationships. But I still hear ignorant strangers—and even people I know and love who were also hurt by the abuse and its effects on an entire community—try to convince me that I "wanted it," that I was at fault. Because of those ill-informed views, the abuser's other victims have refused to come forward, fearing this kind of unwarranted backlash. And these views are exactly the kind of misconceptions about child sex abuse that we need to dispel to develop children who are hard targets for predators.

10 Myths about Child Sex Abuse

Child sexual abuse is surrounded by myths and misconceptions. Let's address some of the most common myths so you can understand why child sexual abuse is underreported, misunderstood, and confusing to adults and caregivers.

Myth #1: "Kids are so sexual these days, it's no wonder abuse is on the rise."

There is no real evidence that child sexual abuse is on the rise. The reason such abuse seems more prevalent now is because more children are reporting, more adults are listening, and our society is no longer scared of talking about abuse. It has nothing to do with children being overly sexualized or abuse rates increasing.

Our culture may seem to be saturated with more sexuality than ever, but the facts remain: Healthy sexuality is fostered between peers in the same age group. Prepubescent children are not sexual with adults. When an adult has sex with a child, it's abuse. If the child is older—a teenager—and an adult in a position of power manipulates and grooms the child for sex, it's abuse.

What about the stereotype of the girl who "throws herself" at a young, handsome teacher? A schoolgirl crush is a healthy sexual behavior. In fact, many researchers and clinicians believe that teens who openly flirt with people in positions of power are learning sexual boundaries in a safe environment, because the adult is not supposed to respond inappropriately. A healthy adult who understands proper sexual boundaries and risky teen behavior will shut down flirting immediately and make sure that he or she is never in a situation alone with any minor. Predators, on the other hand, will accept the invitation, molest the child, and then use the child's insecurity about flirting as leverage to ensure that the child never reports.

A good example of this flirting and an inappropriate response is in the movie *American Beauty*, starring Kevin Spacey and Mena Suvari. Spacey's character lusts after a teenage girl, played by Suvari, who claims to be sexually experienced and openly flirts with Spacey's character. If this middle-aged man were a healthy adult who understood sexual boundaries, he would make sure that Suvari's character was not in the house overnight and never in any room with him alone. Instead Spacey's character pushes sexual boundaries with the girl, who crumbles and cries at his advances. The fact that she is a child becomes clear, and Spacey's character backs off—though in real life, of course, we can't count on a predatory adult suddenly coming to his or her senses and deciding not to abuse.

Myth #2: "Children can't sexually abuse."

Regrettably, this is not the case. In fact, according to a recent study in the UK and Ireland and a 2009 study by the US Department of Justice, approximately one-third of child sexual abuse is committed by someone under age eighteen.[4] Even more tragic, most children who sexually abuse do not get appropriate therapeutic help. If arrested before age eighteen, juvenile offenders' records are sealed. Without immediate intervention, the abusing child will most likely become an abusing adult. Child predators do not suddenly turn predatory as adults. Studies and interviews of child sex predators show that many of these men and women abused, experienced abuse, or harmed other children long before they became adults.

Myth #3: "If my child is abused, we shouldn't tell anyone."

As a victim, I understand that it is hard and humiliating to talk about abuse. But it is even harder for the victim when the subject becomes taboo. Victims need and want to process what happened to them, and the earlier this takes place, the better for the child. While you certainly don't want to take an ad out in the local paper, you *do* want to talk to the victim when the victim wants to talk. You don't want to treat the crime as though it's shameful, embarrassing, or a "secret." Healing comes when victims are able to speak about the crime on their own terms and in a therapeutic setting and are not silenced by people who are embarrassed, ashamed, scared, or angry.

Myth #4: "The legal process is bad for child victims of abuse."

Prosecutors want to put child molesters behind bars. They know, as do victims, that the only way to stop abuse is to punish the perpetrators. But that can't happen if parents don't let their children testify in court.

Over the past thirty years, law enforcement has made huge strides to ensure that children who go through the legal system are not victimized all over again. Groups like the Gundersen National Child Protection Training Center have trained tens of thousands of first responders across the country, helped implement child-friendly interview tactics, and educated lawmakers and judges on how to properly interview a child who is a victim of abuse. Gone are the days of the McMartin Preschool trial, when defense lawyers could show that interview tactics were flawed and law enforcement may have coached the children into pointing fingers.

If you make the decision for your child *not* to pursue criminal charges, you may be allowing a predator to hurt more children. When your child grows up and understands the consequences of that decision, he or she may feel at fault for "allowing" the other children to be abused and the abuser to escape unpunished. Don't put that burden on your child.

Myth #5: "Abusers are easy to spot because they are creepy looking."

If child sex abusers were all creepy or looked like our stereotype of molesters, child molestation would not be a problem. We would be able to tell exactly who the predators are and make sure they were never near our children. But that is not the case. You may feel sure that you would never let a child molester into your family's lives, but chances are that you have already met someone who sexually abuses children. You have shaken that predator's hand. Met him at church. Sat next to her at the beach. Watched him play softball at the park.

Men and women who abuse children are likely to be charming, engaging, and charismatic. They relate to children easily and can talk to a child on a child's own level. They are well liked and attract both adults and children. They get jobs where they are more likely to encounter children who are under their care and supervision. Many times, they assume positions of power over children, making the children more likely to comply with grooming and abusive behaviors. They are great conversationalists, dynamic speakers, and people that you love to be around. They are famous actors, dedicated volunteers, loving family men, doting mothers, and beloved clergymen. In other words, you love them just as much as the children do.

Remember: A predator can be anyone.

Myth #6: "My child is smart enough to walk away from an abuser."

Children are vulnerable. You may think your child is "too smart" to get into a bad situation, but even the smartest teen often lacks the maturity and decision-making skills to escape from the grooming tactics of a predator. The only way your child can become empowered against abuse is for you to be alert and to teach the skills, communication, and tactics necessary to make sure a predator cannot groom your child.

Being a victim has nothing to do with intellect. It has to do with vulnerability. A predator who can discover and capitalize on your child's vulnerability will defeat all the intellect and reason your child can muster. Teach your child about grooming, and give your child tools so he or she is less likely to get into bad situations in the first place.

Myth #7: "Women don't abuse kids."

It's time to put away the "hot for teacher" myth forever. Our culture has tried to tell boys that they grow into "real men" if they are "broken in" by an older woman. But when an adult woman in a position of power has sex with a child or teen, it is not a rite of passage. It's sexual abuse. I have worked with dozens of men and boys who were abused by adult women, and they suffer the same shame, guilt, anger, and self-loathing as victims of abuse by men. And because they are told that they should be proud instead of recognizing their experience as abuse, these victims are even more scared and confused as they grow into adulthood.

Women can also abuse girls. Girls, especially young teens, develop deep friendships with their peers. They easily form strong emotional bonds and look up to women they admire. When a female predator grooms a girl into that kind of deep emotional bond, it's a short leap into sexual abuse. This does not mean that the girl is a lesbian any more than boy victims of male predators are gay. In fact, like all victims, a girl being sexually abused by a woman is often conned into thinking that the sexual activity isn't sex at all, but a way that adults show their love and relate to one another. No matter the method, the abuse is still damaging to the victim, and it's still a crime.

Myth #8: "Children who are sexually abused will go on to be offenders themselves."

This misconception about the tendency of victims to become abusers is called *recidivism*, and it is a particularly pernicious myth. Yet studies have shown that children who are sexually abused are not more likely to become offenders than children who are not abused. A few studies have shown a related tendency in reverse: that men who offend against children have a slightly higher incidence rate of having been sexually abused themselves as children. But on the whole, recidivism is rare. Children who are sexually abused—and get therapeutic care and healing—can grow into healthy, non-offending adults.

Myth #9: "Real victims fight back."

A small percentage of child sex abuse happens under physical force or threat. But child molesters are cunning; they seldom have to hold down a child in order to sexually molest him or her. Their weapons of manipulation, misplaced trust, and twisted love are far more effective than physical force. It is unfair to expect that children can just "fight back" when a trusted adult attempts to sexually abuse them.

A majority of victims—myself and 99 percent of the victims with whom I have worked—were considered "compliant" victims. That means when the abuse started, we didn't say no and didn't fight back. And it's one of the primary reasons that child victims do not report abuse: We were made to believe we wanted it, even though nothing could be further from the truth.

I was convinced until I was almost thirty years old that I must have "asked for" the abuse. What happened to me could not have been rape, I thought, because my perpetrator didn't hold me down or put a knife to my throat. It wasn't until I became an adult that I realized the abuse wasn't my fault and that the weapons my abuser used—grooming and power—were far more effective than a gun or knife would have been. Toddlers, prepubescent children, and teens all fall into this same trap. Whatever the age, when a cunning predator grooms and manipulates a child for sexual abuse, the child becomes a so-called compliant victim.

Once we understand that "fighting back" isn't as easy as it sounds, we can help more victims come forward. If a child believes that he or she will be blamed for the abuse (as I was when I came forward), that child will remain silent. If we outwardly blame child victims who don't fight off their abusers, we allow men and women who sexually abuse children to get a free pass. We cannot assume that a child or teen has any control over an adult in a position of power. And after a predator grooms a child, victims have few (if any) defenses at all. Child sexual abuse is a crime in the eyes of the law and according to common sense. Don't blame the child victim.

A related myth also inhibits the reporting of child sexual abuse: *If the child felt physical pleasure, it's not sex abuse.* A child, especially male, can be confused about the pleasure he may have received from the abuse. If a child molester fellates a child to ejaculation, the action feels good at the moment—even though the child is scared, ashamed, and confused by what is happening. Because the boy had a physical reaction, he may think that his body "liked" it and so he can't report it as abuse. Predators count on that and work hard to make sure that at least some part of the abuse is physically pleasurable to the child.

Myth #10: "Child sexual abuse is about sex."

Child sexual abuse, like all sexual assault, is about one thing: power. It has nothing in common with healthy sexuality, love, mutual pleasure, or an equal relationship. That is why we see mass rape in times of war. It isn't about the soldiers receiving sexual satisfaction from a willing partner—it is about destroying the bodies, wills, and spirits of citizens of the opposing country. It is about using power to defile what the enemy soldier needs and loves the most: his family.

This is also why we see the rape of children in areas where guerrilla warfare and tribalism are rampant. In Liberia, Afghanistan, the Democratic Republic of the Congo, and other countries wracked by civil war, children have been taken from their homes by soldiers who raped and sodomized then to demonstrate complete power over them.

Then, when those same children are handed guns and become soldiers themselves, they in turn use rape to render their enemies powerless.

Child sexual abuse in noncombat regions is similar. A predator uses grooming instead of a gun to render a victim powerless. It has nothing to do with sex and nothing to do with the child's purity, previous actions, or lifestyle.

Signs and Symptoms of Abuse

Now that we have uncovered the myths, let's talk about some facts: what you need to look out for when it comes to child sexual abuse.

The warning signs and symptoms of child sexual abuse are as varied as the victims. But there are some typical behaviors that parents and caregivers should be aware of and take care to address. A victim probably will not exhibit all the behaviors listed here, and many symptoms can indicate problems other than sexual abuse.

The red flags that may signal sex abuse include:

- Nightmares
- Bed-wetting
- Bloody or inappropriately soiled underwear
- Bruising, swelling, or soreness around genitals
- Talking about secrets that can never be revealed
- Fear of being around certain adults
- Depression
- Anxiety
- Anger
- Cutting parts of the body
- A major or sudden change in temperament

- Receiving gifts and money from unknown persons
- Sexualized language
- Playacting sexual activity
- Drawing disturbing images
- Dropping hints to an adult or other child about abuse, troubles, or concerns
- Making inappropriate, sexualized comments in casual discussion
- Alcohol and drug use
- Running away
- Seclusion
- Rapid weight gain or loss

In my own case, I suffered from an escalation of the depression that I had suffered for years. I also secluded myself from my friends, dropped hints to my parents, and lost a great deal of weight. My parents, who were grappling with their own issues surrounding my mother's alcoholism, didn't realize that their child was hurting.

Many of the male victims with whom I have worked didn't descend into depression and isolation. Instead they directed their anger outward, becoming aggressive and reckless, and engaging in high-risk behavior. Many developed an addiction and suffered from violent tendencies and hair-trigger tempers.

Not all victims show symptoms. There are many victims of abuse who show few or no symptoms. But that does not mean the pain is not ever-present in the child's or adult's soul.

If you see any of these behaviors, stop everything and address them with your child. Do not be confrontational or angry. Stay calm, show your genuine concern, and ask questions. Get your child help.

Healthy Sexual Behavior in Children

Although children are not sexual, they often show healthy sexual behaviors in a developmentally appropriate way. Researchers and child development experts have studied these in depth and now realize that it is healthy for children to show some sexual behaviors. There is cause for alarm only when these behaviors become dangerous, when force is involved, or when a child behaves inappropriately even after being told to stop.

The National Sexual Violence Resource Center has a great chart[5] for parents who are concerned about their child's sexual behavior and development. It explains that children from ages two to five have a healthy curiosity about their bodies and the bodies of their parents. They lack inhibition and may enjoy being naked in front of other children. They may also masturbate as a soothing behavior—and this is not a sexual act any more than sucking their thumb is. The chart goes on to explain that children in early elementary school relish potty humor, to point out that preteens tend to seek privacy because of their rapidly (and sometimes awkwardly) changing bodies, and to describe other healthy behaviors. It stresses that healthy behaviors *never* include hurting another child, forcing another child into painful or humiliating actions, or sexual abuse of any kind.

Recognize that your child can engage in developmentally appropriate sexual behaviors. Know what those behaviors are, and do not use shame when addressing them. These are great first steps you can take to understanding when those behaviors are *not* healthy—or to identifying signs that a child is being sexually abused.

Chapter 2

The Perils of Parenting:
Looking in the Mirror

Being a parent is hard. Being a *good* parent is a difficult and evolving process. Being a *perfect* parent is impossible. No one expects you to be perfect. But by picking up and reading this book, you are taking action to safeguard your child and striving to be the best parent you can be. That's exactly what your child needs.

Your Role: Quit Worrying and Start Communicating

The first thing you need to do is take your past and set it aside. This is not about you or what may have happened to you in your life. At the same time, take the "parenting guilt" that we all carry around and toss it aside, too—for a moment, at least. We spend much of our time as parents feeling guilty for what we have or haven't done for our children: *My kids watch too much TV . . . They are way too overscheduled . . . They do not have enough scheduled activities . . . They spend too much time on schoolwork . . . I didn't go over math every day with them this summer . . . I don't read to my kids enough . . . My children spend too much time on the computer . . . I let my kids play too much when they should be reading . . .* And on and on and on . . . Guilt is a self-esteem killer, and it sucks us all in at one time or another. But in most cases, as in the case of child sex abuse prevention, it will do you no good.

We all have made mistakes and dodged some serious bullets while raising children. Once in a while, we didn't dodge those bullets in time. That's in the past, however, and we're setting the past aside. So consider today a fresh new start. No matter your home situation until now, you can make changes to improve your family life and your communication with your child.

All the information in this chapter did not come "out of the blue." In my interviews with hundreds of victims, I have always discussed what their home situation was like before, during, and after the abuse. Certain red flags begin to stand out time and time again. Predators target vulnerable kids. We already know that. But here's what makes this especially bad news: The primary reason a child is vulnerable is because of that child's parents and the role they played—or didn't play.

Sometimes the vulnerability is obvious, such as when a child is physically abused or neglected by his or her parents. A child in the foster care system is also particularly vulnerable. But most of the time, that vulnerability is much more subtle. In my own case, the weak point was my alcoholic mother. She also suffered from a severe and undiagnosed mental illness. My father, my sister, and I were unknowingly enabling her problem. We honestly thought—because of the way she manipulated us—that *we* were the problem. What's more, my father was in denial. He didn't want to believe that the woman he loved with all his heart could at one moment be amazing . . . and the next moment be hateful, hurtful, and destructive. And because we enabled my mother and her behaviors, no one outside of the house knew there was a problem.

Parents who are disengaged also can leave a child exposed to abuse. They may be outwardly happy as a family even though both parents spend all of their time at work, involved in projects, socializing, or volunteering—with a focus anywhere except on the child. This kind of disengagement crosses all socioeconomic levels. We all have heard stories of the megawealthy family in which the parents considered the children just another possession. We also know about the poor or single-parent family with parents who work multiple jobs and, when they are finally home, are too tired to truly engage with their children. I have worked with abuse victims whose parents are in the 1 percent of the 1 percent—children who were flown on private planes for ski vacations and given the best of everything. I have also worked with victims whose parents could not afford to put food on the table.

The point is, it's not a matter of economics or social status. All of these victims told me about their friends who were in the same economic situation. The megarich victims had friends who were as wealthy and as economically spoiled as they were; the poor or single-parent victims said the same. But these friends were not targeted, and the victims knew why: Their friends' parents were engaged in their children's lives. The engaged parents talked to their children, even when they were exhausted from a long day working two jobs. The engaged parents knew who their children's friends were and knew the parents of their children's friends. The engaged parents behaved like adults who loved and cared for their children, intervening when necessary and stepping back when appropriate. The engaged parents listened for cues from their children, even if they had only an hour a day with their children before bedtime. Don't get me wrong: There are plenty of good parents whose kids have been abused or are in danger of being abused. But kids who have great relationships with their engaged parents are far more likely to report the problem right away.

You are your child's first defense. You are also your child's model, hero, advocate, and protector. Hopefully, this chapter can get you started on the right track to engaging in genuine communication with your child—or can reinforce the amazing work you are already doing to keep your child safe.

The Plague of Fear

I speak with parents all the time. Whether I am presenting to a group or chatting at my son's school, I can spot the fear-mongers a mile away: *I don't let my children out of my sight. Did you hear about that child abducted in Texas? I couldn't believe it. So I sat my children down and I told them never to talk to strangers. Then, when they released that one sex offender from jail, I made my children look at his picture. I told them that if they see him, they should scream. It's so awful that my children have nightmares every time there is a story on the news.* Of course the children have nightmares. They are living in a culture of fear.

This is not to say that you should ignore your local Megan's Law website (or other law enforcement site that lists the names and addresses of convicted sex offenders in your area). These websites are wonderful tools that keep communities warned about potential risk. Being proactive and knowing who the offenders are in your area are important actions that can protect your child and others in the area. You can be proactive without cultivating fear in yourself or your child. The purpose of this book is to give you the tools to identify and stop the 90 percent of predators who are never arrested or convicted. Megan's Law–type websites are a terrific companion to the information in this book. To borrow another old cliché: Knowledge is power.

Our children and our society are much better informed than we all were even fifteen years ago. While some kinds of child sex crimes have increased (especially those involving the Internet and child sex trafficking), I believe—and many other victims agree with me—that our children are safer from sex abuse now because we *do* talk about it. More children who are abused report. More children who report are believed. And more predators are put behind bars. Using the simple tools in this book will make your child far less likely to become a target.

A child who lives in fear is a huge target for predators. A child who is scared will trust an adult—*any* adult—to protect him or her. A child who absorbs his parents' fears will not be self-confident. A child without confidence will not understand or push back when he or she is being groomed. That child will not have the tools to succeed against any foe, let alone a cunning adult whom the child knows and has been taught to trust.

So what do you do about this plague of fear? Turn off the TV. Quit reading stories on the Internet about children who have been abducted. Instead, take your child with you to volunteer your time helping others. Make a tangible difference in your world. Not only will you get rid of the paralyzing fear, but you will also give you and your child the power and self-confidence you both need.

Self-Confidence and Your Child

Let's look at the difference between self-confidence and self-esteem and how, for the purposes of this book, we will address them differently.

Self-confidence is a person's outward assurance in how they act, perform, and interact with peers and others. *Self-esteem* is how a person feels about him- or herself. These terms are parallels to *guilt* and *shame*. *Guilt* is what a person feels when he or she has done something bad. *Shame* is what a person feels when that person believes that he or she *is* bad.

It is possible to have guilt without shame. For example, if you have a terminally ill pet that is in a great deal of pain, you may decide to put the pet to sleep. When you do, you most likely will feel guilty, because no one likes to make this difficult decision. But you probably will *not* feel ashamed. You will not feel as though you are a "bad person," because you did the humane and compassionate thing and allowed your vet to ease your pet's suffering. Likewise, it is possible to have self-confidence without self-esteem. While it is not necessary to dive any further into the subtle differences between the two, you need to be able to see when your child lacks either one so you can address the problem in a compassionate and parental way.

A self-confident child is a child who has strong boundaries. These boundaries, which are both physical and behavioral, are vitally important not only in helping your child safely grow in his or her environment, but helping your child thrive safely.

Self-confidence cannot be artificial. Kids are smarter than that. When they get awards for things they didn't earn, are allowed to advance to levels they didn't achieve, or are given compliments they don't deserve, kids see right through it. They don't gain confidence; they feel as though they are being patronized. It's the same for children without boundaries. When children are not appropriately and consistently punished for breaking rules, their lives have no structure. They live in chaos, and they are not made stronger by the experience. Instead they feel alone, insecure, scared, and vulnerable. They may act like a bully, cower in a corner, or become "the quiet kid." But they don't have self-confidence because they don't have confidence in their surroundings.

A child without confidence in his or her surroundings is a vulnerable child who may look for an adult figure to provide insight and stability. Sometimes that child is lucky and finds a good adult who truly cares about the child. Sometimes that child finds a predator.

A child without self-esteem is a completely different animal. A child who is riddled with shame, hates him- or herself, or feels worthless can't be helped solely by structure, love, and positive adult figures. This child needs to learn his or her self-worth through action, interaction, or therapy. If your child has low self-esteem or suffers from depression, talk immediately to your child and explore ways to provide help. You can get a referral to a child therapist from your child's school, the American Psychological Association, or your pediatrician. But act sooner rather than later. A child with low self-esteem is especially vulnerable to any adult who flatters and pays special attention to him or her. Addressing the issue will not only empower your child against predators, but will help your child the rest of his or her life. A child's self-confidence will ebb and flow with the pains of puberty, so keep an eye out, even if you don't think your child is prone to esteem issues. Sometimes a simple talk with a parent can offset weeks of inner turmoil.

Why is all this so important? A self-confident child with at least average self-esteem is the child who will not respond to grooming. This child will also be more likely to immediately remove him- or herself from uncomfortable situations. This child will report odd behavior to a trustworthy adult. This child will come to you if he or she is abused or knows about abuse. You want your child to believe that he or she is a good person, worthy of love and confident in his or her decisions. But the real test is this: You want your child to be confident enough to know that when he or she *doesn't* know the answers, you are always there to help.

Self-Confidence Begins at Home

This may be the part of the book that you don't want to read. But you must. Self-confidence begins with the parents and the home situation. Take a long, hard look in the mirror, and if you see unhealthy attitudes and behaviors there, imagine what your child sees.

Get Control of Your Life

If you are in an abusive domestic relationship, get help immediately. Get help for yourself and for your child. This advice is not just for women. Men are abused at much greater numbers than are reported. If you are a man being abused, there is help for you as well.

It's impossible to hide domestic abuse from a child. Your child sees, hears, and witnesses far more than you know. He or she is learning that it's okay to hit or be hit in relationships, and soon—if it hasn't happened already—your child will begin to take on an adult role. In a home where someone is being physically or emotionally abused, a child is unlikely to report when something happens to him or her. Why? The child fears burdening the parent who is the subject of the abuse.

Next to substance abuse, the number one factor affecting the parents of sexually abused children with whom I have worked is domestic abuse. But even homes that are not affected by domestic abuse can make a child more vulnerable to abuse or less likely to report. If you and your partner are prone to shouting matches, angry outbursts, door slamming, screaming, or fights where you and your partner are evenly matched, you need to take a close look at serious change.

Couples fight—it's only natural. Healthy arguments teach your child how to disagree, solve problems, and manage their world. But once arguments escalate to where your child becomes scared, intervenes, or runs away, you need to address your communication skills with your partner. And of course, any argument that escalates to physical violence should send up a red flag.

If you want to transfer healthy empowerment strategies to your child to keep him or her safer from abuse, you need to have and exercise those skills yourself. You also need to communicate with others in a way that is approachable, caring, empathetic, and calm.

Likewise, if you have addiction or alcohol issues, get help. Children are not stupid. They often know when their parent has a problem before the parent even recognizes it. If you are drunk or high, it makes your child a ripe and easy target—it's as simple as that. Sobriety is not easy, but it is far better than the alternative.

Be a Parent, Not a Friend

Do you consider your under-eighteen child your "best friend"? Do you talk to your child about your marriage or dating relationships or your financial troubles? If so, you are blurring the boundaries of the parent-child relationship and forcing your child into situations that he or she is not equipped to handle. This can make your child feel powerless and undermine his or her self-esteem. It's time to reconsider.

You are a parent. Your child has friends and doesn't need you to be one; your child needs you to be a parent. When you confide adult situations to your child, you burden your child with stress and information that he or she is not ready to handle. Your child should not share in your marriage woes; he or she should feel free to come to you for adult advice, care, guidance, and protection. You don't want your child confiding secrets to a predator because your child lacks a clear-cut parent-child relationship or, like all children, craves someone to set boundaries. You don't want your child living in fear of "burdening you" with his or her problems. Once you start to treat your young child as a peer, that child will lose the parent he or she needs so badly.

You are the adult. Being a parent is your role. That is what your child wants and needs.

Giving Your Child Age-Appropriate Freedoms

We have established that giving your child "free reign" is not a useful goal. Your child needs boundaries in order to develop self-confidence and self-esteem. Within these boundaries, however, allowing your child certain age-appropriate freedoms is vitally important. Hovering or "helicopter parenting" does not allow your child to learn decision-making and other life skills. A child who is awarded appropriate freedoms (which can be taken away because of bad behavior) usually grows into a confident child who is better able to handle all kinds of situations with adults, peers, and younger children. If a parent is constantly there to intervene and tell a child how to act or react, the child will not be able to make proper decisions once he or she is left alone. You want your child to grow and mature in decision-making. If you follow the strategies in this book, you can more confidently send your child out into the world without fear that he or she will fall into the hands of a predator.

The Importance of Free Play

Allowing ample time for free play—play that is not organized, does not involve technology, and is not run by an adult—is important to your child's development. Free play teaches your child how to manage among his or her peers—how to make decisions, solve disagreements, and cooperate. It offers your child the opportunity to be creative. Free play is also when children confide in one another, build friendships, and share life experience. As long as you are well aware of where your child is, who belongs to your child's peer group, and who else may be close by, free play will help your child grow in confidence and without fear. If you do not live in an area where you feel free play is safe, or if your child does not have a close peer group, do your best to find safe places for your child to experiment with play. Also encourage your child to be creative and to entertain him- or herself. Teach your child how *not* to be bored and how to be engaged in and aware of his or her surroundings.

The Privacy Fallacy

Predators capitalize on situations where parents allow their children to enjoy unmonitored and inappropriate privacy. While all children—especially those going through puberty—need appropriate privacy when it comes to their bodies, complete privacy is a casualty that you and your child cannot afford.

For many parents, this is when things get tough. You must reserve the right to go through your child's cell phone, email, and social network accounts. Be sure that this rule is perfectly clear to your child before allowing him or her any of these technologies. If you tell your child that you are doing it for his or her safety, you may get some pushback. But this is where you have to stay strong.

Predators are using technology more and more to groom children, set up meetings, and get kids to send suggestive or nude photos. I've seen teachers, coaches, family members, and other trusted adults use technology to gain unsupervised access. Make sure you know all passwords. Frequently scan your child's phone—unannounced—for inappropriate messages and texts. Do not allow computers in your child's room. Do not allow your child to erase Internet histories. Do not allow your child to play multiplayer games over the Internet, join any kind of "chat room" (even the Disney and Nickelodeon chat rooms are havens for predators), or download games without your approval. If your child is under eighteen, you are responsible for everything he or she posts and sends using various accounts and hardware. There are many back doors for predators, and you are your child's first defense.

Teachers, coaches, and other adults should never directly text students or accept texts from students. If a coach demands to be able to contact your child directly about changes in practice schedules and so forth, tell the coach to text you so you can relay the message. If a teacher is emailing your child about homework, make sure you can read the emails and are copied on all correspondence. Encourage your child's teachers to use message boards that you can access. Ten years ago, a teacher would never allow a student to call him or her at home. We need to create those same boundaries now that technology has put direct communication into the hands of our children.

In the past five years, I have dealt with numerous cases of abuse by trusted adults—usually teachers and coaches—that started with "innocent" texting that then became sexualized. Consider your child's phone like a bedroom: You would not allow your child and a teacher or coach to sit in a bedroom with the door closed, right?

Know who your child is texting, monitor those texts, and keep tabs on your child's computer access and email. It is your job—and no one else's—to make sure your child is protected against would-be predators. Yes, your child requires and deserves a level of privacy that increases with age and development, but not at the expense of his or her safety and protection—and certainly not when it comes to technology.

Stressing Accountability

Protecting your child does not mean shielding your child from accountability. If your child is in trouble at school, on the job, or on the playground, the greatest lesson you can teach your child is to take responsibility for his or her actions. Allowing your child to pass the buck or blame others does not teach accountability. If you don't follow through with consequences—or worse, if you provide no consequences at all—your child does not understand that his or her actions affect people. This can lead to disaster later in life.

Avoid running interference for your child. If your immediate reaction to bad news is, *My daughter would* never *do that* or *I didn't see my son do that, so it didn't happen*, it will give your child the impression that you will always get him or her out of trouble. More important, it will reinforce for your child the importance of *not* telling you the truth about situations. If your child believes that something is okay as long as you didn't see it or don't know the whole truth, then your child will be less likely to tell you when bad things do happen.

Taking this one step further, a child in the clutches of a predator may think that since you didn't see the abuse, you won't believe it happened. What benefited your child the other day now has the potential to hurt him or her.

It's also important to demand accountability from your child's friends. If another child hurts yours and you do nothing, then your child may be less likely to come to you when something really bad happens, thinking, *Well, Mom can't do anything about it.* I'm not saying it is your job to punish other people's children, but you can hold those children accountable. You can tell the child's parents about the behavior, ask the child to go home, or tell the child that such behavior is never allowed in your home. You can reinforce the fact that the child will not be welcome back if the behavior continues. And you can demand that the child appropriately apologizes and considers why what he or she did was wrong and hurtful.

Does this always work? No. But it will reinforce to your child that while you do not meddle or interfere, you do demand good behavior and accountability. Your child knows that you will protect him or her when necessary, and your child's friends learn that you are a strong, stable parent who steps in when things get rough but allows the kids to have fun if the rules are followed.

There is another benefit to stressing accountability. A child who understands that there are both good and bad consequences to actions and decisions is a child who will learn how to make good decisions— first by following you, and then by taking your example and learning to trust his or her "gut feelings." How do you teach your child to follow his or her gut? The next chapter will get you started.

Chapter 3

Your Gut: Your Twenty-Two-Foot Brain

I cannot overemphasize the importance of following your gut and teaching your child to trust his or her instincts. Yes, I am talking about your gut: the organ *and* your instinct. And yes, it has *a lot* to do with preventing child sexual abuse, but also with making good life decisions generally, especially in times of confusion or crisis. This chapter will teach you to truly *listen* to your gut and will show you why it's so important.

Why Talk about the Gut?

How many times have you looked back at decisions you've made and said to yourself, *If only I had listened to my gut?* Whether it's about taking a certain action, going to a particular event, or handling an incident at your child's school, your gut instinct is that first little voice you hear—and the one that usually says, *I told you so*, when you make a different decision. Honing your ability to harness your gut feelings and make decisions accordingly may be difficult, but you'll see better and more positive outcomes.

Had any of the teachers at my high school followed their gut, dozens of other children at my high school could have been spared sexual abuse.

Had I followed my gut, I never would have been abused, my friends would not have been hurt by the abuse, and my community would not have been destroyed.

While I do not blame myself for my abuse, I do accept responsibility for not having the strength to follow my gut. And I accept responsibility for the people who were hurt—including myself—because of it.

Almost every victim of abuse I have worked with has shared stories about decisions they made and regretted. These were innocent decisions: going to someone's house, getting into someone's car, accepting a gift or food from someone. Each time, there was something about these decisions that made the victim's gut say, *Hmm. Should I say no and turn around and leave instead?* But each time, for some reason or another, the victim didn't listen. He or she went into a predator's home. Or got into a predator's car. Or accepted a gift from a predator. Knowing you could have made a different choice if you had only listened to your gut is, well, gut-wrenching. It's tragic.

Parents across the country have made decisions that went against their gut instincts, and these decisions put their child in the path of a predator. That's a horrible burden for any parent to bear—and a preventable one.

I certainly don't blame victims who didn't follow their gut. And we can't blame parents who did the same—adults who had that "hinky" feeling but didn't follow through. Blame only makes the situation worse. And after all, we train our children and ourselves from birth to think with our head rather than listen solely to our instincts. We spend a lifetime trying to silence our inner voice and mute what our gut is trying to tell us. Instead we need to change the way we listen.

Following Your Gut

It's no accident that the gut has been influencing decision-making for all of human history. With more than one hundred million neurons, the enteric nervous system in the gut has more neurons than the spinal cord or the peripheral nervous system (the nerves and ganglia that are not part of the brain or spinal cord). That's a lot of neurons. Our gut saves us from injury and early death—just as it saved our ancestor from the tiger that tried to eat him. Our instincts are why we are not extinct. When faced with danger, early man didn't have time to be logical. His brain stem and his gut made the decisions for him.

What worked for him can work for us.

Your Second Brain

Many scientists call your gut the "second brain," and it's the main reason we get butterflies in our stomachs when we are nervous and talk about "gut reactions" to situations and decisions. This second brain is not a highly developed system. It uses *feelings* and *instinct* to guide our thinking. It does this through hormone production and firing neurons, much of the same work your actual brain does. In fact, most of your body's serotonin—a hormone that influences mood and depression—is found in your gut, which explains why your midsection has such a profound impact on your overall sense of well-being. How many of us get a sour stomach when we are nervous or expecting bad news? How many of us become constipated or get diarrhea when we are upset or anxious? You can thank the thinking part of your gut for that.

Your gut works at a simple level—it does not engage in the high-level thinking required for things like speech, problem-solving, or logic. But it does impact decision-making. We have even integrated the role of the gut in our everyday language: How many times have you said, *My gut is telling me this is a bad idea?*

The problem is, we have trained ourselves to shut this second brain down. From the time we enter school, we are trained to use our brains to override instinct. We teach ourselves to rationalize every decision we make, which leaves us easily influenced by peers who can talk us out of any decision. The person with the most words or the loudest voice often wins the argument.

Predators love it when we don't listen to our gut. Why? Because when we see a predator in action, we *rationalize* the actions and make excuses. Thus we might overlook what are in fact the first stages of grooming—the little actions that strike us as a bit odd. Instead of questioning why a man is spending a great deal of time with a fatherless child, we tell ourselves that we are overreacting. Instead of reporting suspected abuse by a teacher to the Childhelp hotline, we tell a school administrator because we have convinced ourselves that an administrator can handle the situation better than we can.

What's worse, we train our children to minimize *their* instincts and the feelings they get from the second brain. We tell our children that they have to hug people who make them uncomfortable. We tell them that they must obey adults. We tell them that stranger danger and abduction are the big things to worry about. When they confide in us that they don't like a certain place or person, we tell them that their feelings are "silly." So what happens? Our children suppress their instincts. As they grow older, this suppression continues and grows.

We don't mean to kill our children's instincts, but our society values brain power and logic over intuition. In the case of the gut, we tell our kids that logic is the voice they really need to obey. It's time to change that. Our brains and our guts need to work *together*.

Trusting Your Instinct

Instinct is a powerful tool. Logic didn't save early man from predators like tigers or an angry neighboring clan with spears. Instinct did. We are hardwired through our "fight or flight" system to act quickly in times of danger. Early man instinctively knew to pick up his spear and fight back when he was attacked—an obvious reaction. But he may have gone to bed with his spear next to him because he had an odd feeling—something in his gut that told him the angry neighbors were ready to launch an attack.

What saved early man in this situation can translate to sexual abuse situations now. We need to embrace and nurture that "odd feeling" that tells us something bad is going to happen.

Don't think that gut instincts in parents and children are important? Here is an example: Let's say Nick is an average, outgoing, and likeable ten-year-old boy. He is invited to go on a campout sponsored by a youth organization he regularly attends and loves. But there is a problem: He doesn't want to go. Mr. Jones, one of the volunteer leaders, will be there, and Mr. Jones makes him feel odd. Nick can't put his finger on why, but he doesn't like to be around Mr. Jones, even though the adult regularly takes other boys and his own son to the movies, buys them things, and is good friends with Nick's parents.

Nick tells his parents that he doesn't want to go on the campout. Like most ten-year-olds, he doesn't say why. He just tells his folks, "I'd rather stay home."

"Don't be silly," his mother says. "Mr. Jones will be there, and you love him and his son. It will be great."

"Mr. Jones . . . he . . . well . . . ," Nick replies. "I don't like him a whole lot."

"Since when?" Nick's father interjects. "He and I have been friends for years. Don't say those kinds of things. After everything he has done for you, I find your behavior downright disrespectful. You'll go, and you'll have a good time."

So Nick goes.

The first night of the campout, Mr. Jones takes Nick and another boy to his tent, where he has alcohol. "This is for the real men," Mr. Jones tells the boys.

Nick, too scared to say anything, and following his father's orders, takes a cup.

You can guess what happens next.

The Power of Your Gut

Do you remember how you felt the day your child was born? Remember those "butterflies" you had in your stomach? They were probably nearly as bad the day you got married or started an important job. At times, you may have even been so nervous that you vomited, even though you believed you were making the right decision.

Now think about when you were a child. Did you ever feel physically ill before a big test? Did you have teachers who made you feel happy inside and teachers whose classroom made you break out in a sweat? Your emotions and the input into your brain manifested itself into nausea, vomiting, and unhappiness.

Your brain and your gut are powerful organs that, when upset or scared, can create real physical symptoms. Think about a panic attack; it may be "all in your head," but it sure doesn't feel that way. It feels as though you are having a full-blown heart attack and death is imminent. But your brain and your gut can also be subtle. It's all in how you listen and respond to the signals they are giving you.

The younger you are, the more profound these signals and feelings can be. They are also difficult for a child to explain.

When I was in grade school, I suffered from horrible anxiety. The anxiety, which probably had its roots in my mother's mental health and alcohol issues and in my perfectionism, was something that I didn't understand. To me, I was just a kid who had a hard time getting to sleep and who got horrible chest pains on Sunday nights. Usually they happened just after dinner, when it was time to get things ready for the upcoming school day.

When I went to my parents and told them that my chest hurt, they were skeptical and thought I was trying to figure out a way to stay up late. I really can't blame them—children are quick to make up false ailments when they don't want to go to bed or school or to unload the dishwasher. They told me I was being silly. I was quickly dismissed and told to go and get ready for bed.

My parents had the best intentions. They didn't realize that I was wracked with anxiety, because I didn't know how to tell them. I didn't have the language to express it, and they didn't have the patience to ask the right questions.

No parent is a mind reader, but if my parents had asked me a few questions (especially since my father himself suffered from childhood anxiety), perhaps they could have helped me manage my symptoms. But instead their reaction taught me to dismiss my gut instinct that something was wrong. I thought that anxiety was totally normal and that if someone upset me or made me feel anxious, I just needed to get over it.

By the time I was being groomed for sex abuse, my gut didn't stand a chance. While there were a dozen other reasons that I was targeted, had I been able to say, "This feels wrong. I need to turn around and walk away," I might have spared myself decades of pain.

Teaching Your Child to Trust His or Her Gut

No specific set of lessons can help your child learn to trust his or her gut, but with gentle encouragement and some good modeling, your child can begin to harness the power of his or her instincts.

Talk about Feelings

This is especially helpful for younger children, who still heavily look to their parents for cues on how to behave. In the car, at the dinner table, or in any relaxed situation, talk about how you made a recent decision based on your instincts. It could be about something as simple as, "I had a gut feeling it was going to rain, so I picked up my umbrella just in case."

For older kids, ask questions about situations they may confront with their peers or in school. Ask them about their friends. Ask them about challenges they or their peers face. Ask them about issues: Do they see bullying? Are their peers sexually active? Why do they hate a certain teacher but love another? What scares them? Do they think that adults understand the issues teens face? If there is a "scandal" at the school—cheating, drugs, abuse, or something else—ask them what they know and how they *feel* about it and why. Ask them what they would have done in that situation or why they made the decisions they made. Ask if they have regrets.

If your child clams up, keep trying over time. Most teens will be able to offer no shortage of instances and examples in which their peers should have "followed their gut."

Validate Feelings

Talk about feelings—yours and others'—so your child understands that there's no such thing as "wrong" emotions. Be compassionate, even when you disagree. With younger kids, it's as easy as asking, "Why do you think you feel that way?" Even if your child doesn't have physical pain or a bad feeling, he or she may tell you something worth hearing. But the simple fact that you asked how the child feels and why he or she feels that way will make a big difference later on.

For older kids and teens, all it takes is telling your child you understand it's hard to be a teenager. Because it is. Simply saying, "Being a teen is hard. Sometimes it seems like no one understands," may open up a Pandora's box of information.

Express Feelings

Let your child see that you are open to sharing feelings, and encourage your child to reciprocate. I am not saying your child should be the emotional leader of the household. But recognize that your child wants to be able to tell you how he or she feels, even if that emotional state is tinged with anger.

With older children, reinforce the avenues of communication by asking questions that encourage them to share their emotions. Kids are faced with millions of potential problems throughout the course of the day, so ask them gently what they are feeling. If your child can't tell you why, see if you can find the right questions to help your child figure it out. Not only do you want to be a sounding board, but you also want to teach your child how to handle, understand, and embrace all of his or her emotions. But remember to strike a careful balance between meeting them on their level and empathizing as an adult bystander. Your child does not want to be your peer. Your child wants your guidance, even if he or she is a surly teenager. Victims from Alaska to Florida have told me the same thing: "I screamed at my parents. I told them I hated them. I just wanted them to help me, but I didn't know how to ask."

Your goal is to find that balance, open your ears, and be a parent.

The Gut into Adulthood

Talking to your child about trusting her gut will be a lifelong discussion. As your child begins to expand his horizons—going to college, finding a job, living alone, joining the military, traveling abroad, or starting a family—trusting his or her gut is a skill that will come in handy for assessing situations, making decisions, handling crises, and managing relationships.

If you continually give your child guidance and input—and if you engage in discussion about decision-making, trusting the gut, and understanding accountability for actions—you can send your child off into adulthood with a greater chance of success, confidence, and happiness.

And he or she will be much safer from predators.

Part Two

The Predator

Chapter 4

Grooming: The Predator's Gateway

One of the most complicated aspects of child sexual abuse is explaining the concept of grooming. For an adult who has not been abused, it's a difficult concept to grasp: How can an adult make a child think abuse is okay? How can the abuser persuade the victim not to report the abuse? Why did the victim keep going back? Why did the victim deny the abuse and protect the abuser at first? Why is the victim so ashamed? Why didn't the child scream, "*No!*" and run away? Why didn't the child fight back?

And then there's the most tragic question of all: Why do many child victims love their abusers? The answer is: grooming.

Grooming is the reason that predators get away with decades of abuse without being caught. It's why law enforcement can have a hard time prosecuting crimes. It's why many victims of child sexual abuse grow into adulthood hiding in self-imposed shame and silence.

The concept of grooming can be terrifying, but if you understand it and know what to look for, grooming becomes transparent and easy to spot. This chapter will show you how.

Why Does Grooming Work?

How can a child go against his or her morals or sexuality? How does a predator get a child to do things that are so abhorrent, even to the child? Why do teen boys who identify as straight "allow" themselves to be molested by men? How do abusers ensure that their victims will keep their "secret"? It's all in the grooming. And a predator who uses things like drugs, alcohol, or cunning manipulation can get a child to do or believe just about anything.

The "Compliant" Victim

If you ask a victim of child sex abuse how the predator was able to get close, blur boundaries, and make sure that the child victim didn't shout, fight back, or report, you will probably get an answer like this: *I was groomed.*

But what is grooming? Why don't we know more about it?

Describing grooming is complicated. The easy textbook answer is sterile and doesn't get to the heart of the problem: Grooming is when a predator emotionally and psychologically manipulates a child into becoming a "compliant" victim. Grooming isolates a child from his or her peers and family, and makes the predator the most important person in the child's life.

Let's take a different view, in plain English: Grooming is how a predator tricks a child into believing that sex abuse is okay. It's how a predator uses love and attention to make the child feel special, important, and loved. It's how a predator cons a community into believing that he or she is a wonderful, loving, and outgoing person who would never hurt a child. It's how a predator uses your child's vulnerabilities and insecurities to trick him or her into becoming a so-called compliant victim.

The vast majority—more than 95 percent—of child sex abuse victims are carefully groomed. These children are not held down, threatened with immediate bodily harm, or kidnapped. Most victims continue to see the predator even though they know they will be abused. In that way, they are compliant victims, and a predator will spend months creating the right conditions for compliance.

And even the smartest children are susceptible.

The "Chamber of Secrets": An Example of Grooming

For those who still find it hard to understand how powerful the process of grooming can be and why it works so well, fortunately there is an example that hits the nail on the head. With the story of eleven-year-old Ginny Weasley, from the second book of the Harry Potter series—*Harry Potter and the Chamber of Secrets*—the reader experiences how an adult can use power, flattery, and love to get a child to do *anything he wants*—even if it goes against common sense and the child's innate moral values.

Ginny is a first-year student from a poor family that can't afford to provide all the trappings that her schoolmates have—things like new books, school supplies, uniforms, and clothes. Even so, Ginny's many older brothers have a strong sense of self-confidence, reinforced by loving parents. Ginny, however, is not so lucky.

As the only daughter in a house full of sons, Ginny lacks her brothers' confidence and swagger. Plus, she has a not-so-secret crush on the older Harry Potter, a crush that subjects her to endless ribbing from her older siblings. Away at boarding school, Ginny is totally alone. Her brothers love her, but they don't provide support. Her crush is unrequited. She feels as though no one understands her.

What can solve Ginny's problems? Love and attention. She needs a friend. She needs a confidant and mentor. She needs someone who understands her, listens to her, and validates her. She needs to feel special. She finds that "person" in a magical diary.

The diary comes from what seems to be the "safest" of places:

mixed up in some schoolbooks her parents purchased in a trusted and respected bookstore. Believing the diary is harmless, the girl starts to write. But this is no normal diary. The ink on the page magically disappears as soon as she scribbles her deepest thoughts. And something amazing happens: New words appear—a response from the original owner of the diary, Tom Riddle.

Riddle, who is actually an evil wizard, listens to Ginny's deepest secrets and responds with understanding, something that Ginny does not get anywhere else in her world. He flatters the child and becomes her best friend. For once, she feels special.

Tom Riddle isolates her from other people, telling her that no one would ever understand her, their relationship, or the magic they share. It's a powerful secret, and Ginny thinks there is no one she can tell. Soon, however, things go bad. Ginny unconsciously commits acts of destruction. Some of her classmates are cast under a spell that may kill them. A chamber of secrets is opened, and a deadly beast is unleashed in the school. And Ginny thinks all these things may be her fault . . . because of Tom Riddle and the magic in the diary.

Despite this, she says nothing. How can she? The diary was *her best friend*. She *willingly wrote in it and kept the secret* about Tom Riddle. Scared and confused, she has nowhere to turn. She feels powerless to stop the diary, isolated from her peers, and scared of her own actions. She believes that she has betrayed the people she loves the most—her family and Harry.

Tom Riddle used charm, compassion, secrets, understanding, and lies to get everything he wanted from Ginny. Did Ginny *want* to do horrible things? Did the fact that she didn't tell an adult about the diary mean she was a co-conspirator in the crimes? No. She was carefully groomed. She was an innocent child who was manipulated and enchanted by an evil wizard who wanted to use her for his own ends.

Child sex predators are no different from Tom Riddle and the diary. While the perpetrators are not enchanted wizards, they do possess immense power over a child and can easily create a compliant victim. Ginny was not a willing victim; that is, she didn't want to hurt anyone, keep the secret, or do any of the things she did. *But she was made compliant because she lacked the power and ability to say no, stop the abuse, or tell anyone about it.*

At the end of the book, Ginny's parents find out about the diary. Instead of expressing compassion over what happened to their daughter, they are quick to scold her. In their eyes, she "allowed" herself to be enchanted. By not telling anyone, she condoned the evil. In essence, they blamed her for being vulnerable, for being manipulated and exploited, and for then being too scared and powerless to stop the course of action.

Fortunately for Ginny (and for victims of abuse who read *Harry Potter and the Chamber of Secrets*), the wise wizard Dumbledore schools Ginny's parents. When he tells them that she was powerless over Tom Riddle and the diary, they back down. Dumbledore understood that there is nothing more vulnerable than a child in need of attention and love.

How Does a Predator Groom a Child?

A predatory adult uses flattery, gifts, money, attention, threats, alcohol and drugs, secrets, and confidence to build trust and blur sexual boundaries. The predator takes seemingly innocent things like attention, hugs, and gifts, and twists them into tools of seduction.

After weeks or months of a close but "normal" relationship with the child, the predator will attempt sexualized touching. It will be so slow and so subtle that the child may not even know or remember when everything "changed." Hugs become long hugs. The predator may talk about sexual behavior or say that "real friends" embrace nudity or touching. Kissing becomes longer or focuses on other areas of the body. The predator may tell the child about how "adult" he or she is—how mature, how worthy of love, how sexy. With pubescent children, the predator will talk about masturbation and sexual release being normal and natural, especially when it is done around people . . . like the trusted and loved predator.

The predator may use contraband like pornography, especially with boys, as a "special secret." The predator may give kids alcohol and drugs to lower their inhibitions and to use as leverage if the child threatens to tell: *You did drugs. You broke the rules and you'll be in big trouble. And anyway, who is going to believe anything you say?*

Grooming is a long, slow process, full of subtlety and innuendo. Because the predator has moved very slowly, gauging the victim's response step by step, even a child is conned into believing that the abuse is okay, when he or she is confused, scared, hurt, or ashamed.

Think of how easily adults are conned and hoodwinked by charming, charismatic snake oil salesmen hawking fraudulent products or get-rich-quick schemes. Financial predators like Bernie Madoff conned smart people out of millions of dollars. Don't expect your child to have tools that even smart adults don't have. Children, when faced with a charming adult showering love and attention on them, barely stand a chance.

The Process of Grooming

Grooming takes time, patience, and practice. Think of it as how a predator "dates." Child molesters can't go to bars and meet potential partners. They can't be set up on blind dates. There is no legal or acceptable way for them to find children to sexually abuse. So they must very carefully select a child, determine whether the child is vulnerable, and then slowly begin the abuse.

There is a distinct process to grooming. If we look closely at our example of Ginny Weasley and Tom Riddle, the process becomes clear:

"It's very *boring*, having to listen to the silly little troubles of an eleven-year-old girl," he went on. "But I was patient. I wrote back. I was sympathetic, I was kind. Ginny simply *loved* me. *No one's ever understood me like you, Tom . . . I'm so glad I've got this diary to confide in . . . It's like having a friend I can carry around in my pocket . . .*

"If I say it myself, Harry, I've always been able to charm the people I needed."

First, Tom Riddle gains the girl's trust by listening to her with compassion and without judgment. Soon, she discloses more and more, including her insecurities and secrets. Now armed with Ginny's vulnerabilities, Riddle is able to fill the voids in her life. She wants a friend and wants to feel important. He does that for her . . . and more.

In other cases, the predator may tell the child that he or she is a grown-up, spend quality time with a child whose parents are absent, give the child gifts, take the child places, validate the child's feelings, or claim that he or she loves the child more than the child's parents ever could. By this time, the child loves the predator as a trusted adult.

Predators blur boundaries. In the case of Ginny Weasley, the boundaries were moral, not sexual. Even though she didn't remember doing anything bad, she knew that she had been the culprit of some dangerous things. In the case of sexual abuse, a predator will confuse the child into thinking that sexual behavior is okay, even if it hurts, feels wrong, or causes shame and embarrassment.

Because of her trust in and love for Tom Riddle, it took Ginny a while to realize that she needed to tell someone. Riddle shared his special secrets and crafted a strong bond of trust; she didn't want to betray him. By keeping the diary and her relationship with Riddle a total secret, she had become isolated from her peer groups and trusted adults. She had nowhere to turn, except inward—or to the diary.

This is why so many victims continue to return to the man or woman who abused them. Many times, the predator is the only person whom the child believes he or she can trust. Other times, the child knows the predator's power and is afraid to disobey. Once the child has been isolated and the sexual and personal boundaries have been blurred, the child is the perfect compliant victim, and the abuse begins.

Grooming the Next Victim

For the active predator, maintaining dominance over the abused child while grooming other children can be the most difficult part of the grooming process. Many child molesters have an age "type"; once a victim "ages out" or otherwise outgrows the needs of the predator, the child will be discarded and the predator will move on to another child. Other predators will groom and abuse numerous children at a time. This can be a dangerous time for an active predator, so his or her control of victims is very important. If a victim no longer feels special, he or she is likely to get angry or jealous and report the abuse. To counteract this, many predators use shame and guilt to ensure the victim's silence. Some predators will tell the child that he or she "wanted" the abuse and actually enjoyed it. Other predators will tell the child that no one will believe him or her. Still others use threats of force or pain, whether applied to the victim or to the victim's family members. Threats are rare, however, because most victims are easily silenced through shame and manipulation.

Why Do Predators Groom?

Predators groom for a variety of reasons. The first is that grooming creates a compliant victim who is unable to fight back or say no. Grooming also creates victims who will continue to see and visit the predator, because they are too confused, too scared, or under the predator's "spell." The abuse continues because the child does not know how to make it stop.

Grooming is also self-selective and is used as a "weeding out" method for predators. Child predators do not want to molest children who are likely to fight or object. So they start slowly. After weeks of flattery or gifts, the predator may try to introduce slight sexual touching. A child who has a high level of self-confidence and a complete understanding of body boundaries will object by either saying no, walking away, reporting the behavior, or pushing the predator away. The predator will then move on to the next child, because it's easier to find a more compliant victim than it is to force a confident child to succumb.

The saddest and scariest part is that predators groom victims because predators know that they *can make the child love them.* A vulnerable and isolated child will do anything, even if it's awful, to maintain that love.

Signs of Grooming

It is crucial for you, as a parent, to know the signs of grooming and to talk to your child *before* grooming for sexual abuse begins. These signs are subtle and varied, but a watchful eye will discern the kinds of activity that seem too generous or "over the top." Many of these signs may seem innocent enough, even though they make the little hairs on your neck stand up. Remember, as we discussed in chapter 3, how crucial it is to listen to your gut.

The signs of grooming include, but are not limited to:

- Gifts or money that your child cannot or will not explain
- A special adult friend who showers your child with gifts
- An adult who spends large amounts of time with your child
- An adult who wants to spend "alone time" with your child
- Keeping special secrets with an adult

- Secrecy and mood changes in your child
- An adult who is "too good to be true" and offers babysitting, money, or support to your family
- An adult who offers to "counsel" your troubled child outside of the school or a licensed therapeutic setting
- Messages or texts from an adult to your child
- Your child using an Internet connection or email account that is not monitored by you
- Special consideration given to your child by a teacher or community member
- An adult with no children who comes to child-centric events just to "be around the kids"
- Long hugs, back rubs, or other "slightly inappropriate" touching
- Overnight trips with only one adult and numerous children (related or not related to the adult)
- Spending time with an adult behind closed doors
- A parent's boyfriend or girlfriend who spends too much or inappropriate alone time with your child
- Alcohol or drug use
- Sex talk or evidence of pornography
- An adult who encourages your child to be naked

While some of these activities are big red flags (e.g., sex talk, pornography, nudity), others are more subtle. You will immediately recognize the difference when you speak frankly with the adult who is exhibiting these behaviors: A potential predator may get defensive. He or she may claim to do it with other kids "all the time." The predator may be insulted or try to shame you. But an adult who is harmless will apologize profusely and ask you what an appropriate activity would be.

Victims Who Love Their Abusers

Carefully groomed victims love their abusers. Incest victims understand this better than anyone. I worked with an incest victim who was considering filing criminal and civil charges against her father, a high-ranking official in a private, nonreligious school. Like most groomed victims, she was scared and isolated. Her mother told her that the family would reject her if she talked to the police. But that wasn't the worst part: Even though the victim knew it was the right thing to do, *she didn't want to report her father.* She loved him, telling me, "He's the only father I have." She recounted the good times they had together and as a family, even defending his behavior. The only reason she was going to go to the police, she told me, was because she had reason to believe that her father was molesting another, much younger family member.

Carefully groomed child victims love their abusers the same way. And children who love their abusers are the least likely to ever report the abuse.

The Other Victims of Grooming

Children are not the only victims of grooming. A good predator with many years of experience will know that the best way to get to a child is through the child's family, community, or support system. That's why predators are attracted to jobs that are likely to put them around children and families: coaches, teachers, clergy, Scout leaders. All too often, predators choose an adult boyfriend or girlfriend who has kids.

These predators are charming and engaging. They give the best sermons, are the most empathetic Scout masters, and are the neighborhood guys that all the kids love. Most of the time, they present themselves as a model and loving citizen. And the parents get sucked into the grooming cycle.

Adults, like children, are susceptible to charm and charisma. A successful predator knows that a child whose parents are carefully groomed will not disclose abuse. And if the child does disclose, groomed parents are less likely to believe that child.

Think of it this way: A parent is faced with a child who has exhibited behavioral problems, may be into drugs and alcohol, is isolated from his peers, and is surly and angry. This teen now says that a popular and well-liked youth leader sexually molested him. Whom are the parents more likely to believe? The troubled child with anger and addiction issues? Or the friendly, upstanding youth leader—who, when parents aren't around, gives the kids drugs, porn, and alcohol before he sexually abuses them and then swears the kids to shameful secrecy?

A case that highlights this dynamic is the tragic turn of reality star Honey Boo Boo, a former child beauty pageant contestant who went on to star in her own reality show, *Here Comes Honey Boo Boo*, from 2012 to 2014. Her mother, Mama June, reunited with a boyfriend who is a convicted sex offender—and who, Mama June's older children say, abused them as well. But because Mama June was so groomed and charmed by this man, she was willing to risk everything, including her children's safety, to be with him. Even when the victims reported the abuse and TLC cancelled the show, destroying the family's main source of income, Mama June did not seem to renounce him or what he allegedly did to her daughters. This may be a case where a parent simply refuses to believe the stories of abuse because she had been so carefully groomed.

How to Prevent Grooming

The number one thing you can do to be sure that your child is not groomed for sexual abuse is to engage with your child—talk, interact, and care. (See chapter 2 for more on this.) Predators groom children who need adult attention and who are aching for validation, love, and support. Give your child that attention and love so he or she does not seek it elsewhere.

Talk to your child, starting when he or she is very young. Ask open-ended questions about the adults in your child's life. Ask about what your child sees and observes. Don't dismiss any fears, opinions, or anger your child expresses about his or her world.

There are also more tangible things you can do to help not only your child, but also your child's peers. More age-specific strategies will be discussed in later chapters, but this is a good place to start:

- Identify the trusted adults in your life. Talk to them about sexual abuse and your rules concerning your child.

- Reinforce your child's body boundaries at every stage of his or her life.

- Tell your preteen or teen that no adult should ever give him or her drugs, alcohol, or pornography. Reinforce that it's okay for your child to tell you or a trusted adult if this ever happens.

- If your child receives gifts from an adult that you consider inappropriate, return the gifts to the adult.

- Help your child build self-confidence and self-esteem through activities that he or she likes.

- Talk openly and in an age-appropriate manner about sexuality, puberty, and development. Answer your child's questions, especially if the child develops much earlier or later than his or her peers.

- Address body issues such as acne, weight gain, size, beauty, and social issues such as being in a certain clique. Reinforce the fact that your child is beautiful and is growing and changing every day, and that you support and respect your child's personality and intelligence.

- Do not try to be a "friend." Be a strong and loving parent who is open and compassionate. That's what your child needs most.

- Talk to your child in an age-appropriate way about what defines a proper relationship between an adult and a child and an adult and a teen.

- Monitor your child's peer group, and make sure your child is not isolated or bullied. If your child is being bullied, address the situation immediately.

- Enact the two-to-one rule: There should always be at least two adults present so your child is never alone with just one adult (except for adults you trust beyond a doubt). Tell your child it's a safety rule, like looking both ways when crossing the street.

- Monitor the adults who are involved in your child's life.

- Immediately address red-flag behavior from a coach, teacher, neighbor, or other adult.

- Monitor your child's technology, including Internet, cell phones, social media, and email. Do not allow children to use Internet-enabled devices in their rooms.

- Look at yourself in the mirror and identify behaviors you may have that may alienate your child.

- Embrace your child's sexual identity. Ensure that if your child is struggling, the adults in his or her life are strong role models who will not take advantage of your child's confusion or shame in order to groom and molest.

There is no failsafe way to ensure that a child will not be targeted. As we saw with Ginny Weasley, even smart children with loving parents can be ensnared. But a child who has strong, safe relationships with adults, self-confidence, self-esteem, and a concrete sense of boundaries is less likely to be targeted in the first place.

Chapter 5

Who Is the Predator?
Beyond the Stereotypes

Not everyone is a predator—but anyone can be a predator. It's a tough reality to accept, but as a parent you must accept it in order to keep your child safe.

This chapter is not about panic-mongering, however. It's not about teaching you to look at every person with suspicion. So stop watching the news. Stop cruising the Internet. Get off the Megan's Law websites and sex offender registries. Take a deep breath. The fact that you are reading this book puts you in the top percentage of empowered and educated parents. Your child is *already* safer.

Chances are that your child will not be sexually abused by an adult in a position of power. But chances are that your child knows someone who already has been abused. And chances are that the person came from the most unlikely of places. That's the key takeaway for this chapter: Most predators come from the places we least expect.

Predators Rely on Stereotypes

Predators want you to believe that it's only the dirty old man in the trench coat who molests children. They don't want you to realize that predators can be handsome and successful. They don't want you to know that predators can be men *or* women. They want to keep you in the dark about the fact that teens—and even younger children—can abuse, and that successful predators have hidden behind their roles as loving parents, engaged community leaders, winning coaches, and inspirational holy leaders.

Uncovering abuse and the predators who commit abuse means breaking down assumptions and removing stereotypes. Keeping your child safe means understanding that abusers can take any shape or form—even that of a beloved friend, neighbor, or family member. In fact, even if you or someone you love is *not* a victim of abuse, you may face another heartbreaking problem: what to do when someone you know, love, or respect is accused of abuse.

The Opposite of Creepy

I have already told you who the predator most likely *isn't*: the creepy guy in the trench coat. In fact, most often, we aren't talking about anyone creepy at all. Children don't like creepy people and will not spend time with them. We are talking about someone who *attracts* children and who knows exactly what they want and need to feel special. Predators want their victims to love them, and for that to happen, they must be *lovable*. Even if the predator isn't the warm, fuzzy type, he or she needs to have ways to relate to kids. Because if a predator cannot attract and relate to children, a predator can't find victims.

As we discussed in chapter 4 about grooming, a predator also needs to appear lovable and charming to adults. Think about the last time you heard about someone being accused of abuse, whether it was a celebrity, a sports figure, a community member, or a teacher. If the story was covered in the media, what was the most common quote you heard? Probably something like, *Oh, Mr. So-and-so would never hurt a child. He is a wonderful man and very well-respected. Everyone loves him, and the children admire him. I would trust my children with him anytime. Anyone accusing him of abuse just wants attention and money.*

It's a familiar refrain that many victims hear when they come forward and report abuse. Charming and well-respected community members, celebrities, and sports heroes are exactly the kinds of people who can entice and groom children. And of course, when anticipating the kinds of reactions like the one I just outlined, these children are unlikely to come forward unless another victim leads the way.

An example is the scandal involving comedian Bill Cosby. After a video of comedian Hannibal Buress went viral, in which he cited previous allegations against Cosby and called him a rapist, more than two dozen women have come forward to say that Cosby drugged and raped them when they were young actresses breaking into the business. Allegations against Cosby had been floating around for years, but it took another person's remarks to make it "safe" at last for the victims to come forward with their stories. If it took adult women decades to talk publicly about what happened to them, think about how a child must feel when in the same position.

Nobody wanted to believe that the beloved, iconic Cosby could commit such widespread abuse. But that is the case all too often—the predator turns out to be the "cool teacher," the "awesome youth director," the "engaging minister," or the "best troop leader our boys have ever had." That's why it is so important not to allow yourself to be groomed into ignoring your gut. And that's why you should never dismiss your child's instincts, even when someone you really like makes your child feel odd or strange, or does things that your child does not like.

Women Who Abuse Children

Women are our mothers and grandmothers. They are our stereotypical caregivers and nurturers. They love and raise children, protect them from harm, and soothe them when they are sick or in pain. The idea of women hurting children is hard for many people to stomach. We want to believe that sexual abuse goes against a woman's DNA.

But we need to face it: Women can also abuse.

Stereotypes of the loving mother have allowed women predators to thrive—and even be celebrated—in popular culture. Unfortunately, their victims still suffer. Look at movies like *Porky's* and songs like Van Halen's "Hot for Teacher," which celebrate the young boy who is "broken in" by the hot, oversexed adult woman. What they don't explore, however, is how damaging this abuse is to the male victims, who are isolated from their peers, thrust into adulthood, manipulated, groomed, and then left with nowhere to turn for help.

Abuse by women is hardly new, but only in recent years have reports been on the rise. This is probably due to a number of factors, including public outrage at the crimes of thirty-five-year-old wife and mother of four Mary Kay Letourneau. Her victim was not a thirty-year-old actor playing a seventeen-year-old boy looking to break into manhood, as in a movie like *Porky's*. He was a sixth-grader who was repeatedly molested by his teacher. She was jailed twice for molesting the boy. Although the couple is now married with children, one can hardly view their relationship as healthy.

Letourneau is a shining example of a predator masquerading as a trustworthy adult. Not only was she a teacher, but she was married with children who were close in age to the boy she was sexually molesting. We can only assume that she knew what she was doing was wrong, though she justified her actions—as all predators do—by call-ing it "love" or "fate." In a 2011 interview with ABC's Barbara Walters, Letourneau said she would not approve of her twelve-year-old daugh-ters dating their teachers.

Once the Letourneau story made it "okay" for these victims to come forward, the boys and girls molested by women began to speak out. Suddenly, "Hot for Teacher" wasn't really cool anymore, and vic-tims felt safe to say that being sexually abused by an adult woman was terribly damaging.

When you look at arrest statistics, the vast majority of predators are still men. But women are being arrested and punished at much higher rates as time passes. This is good news. Remember, women have been abusing all along—they didn't just suddenly get the notion that abuse would be a good idea. But now that the police are taking victims seri-ously and victims feel empowered to come forward, these women are being punished at much higher rates.

Another thing to remember: Like male predators, women pred-ators target vulnerable kids. Some of the most vulnerable are those struggling with their sexual identity (an issue we will talk about in chapter 12). Women target girls as often as they target boys. They use all of the same grooming tactics to isolate a child, blur boundaries, and sexualize the relationship.

Family Members Who Abuse Children

A family is supposed to provide a safe haven for its members, but sometimes home is the last place a child feels secure about turning to.

It's sad but true that a great amount of sexual abuse happens in the family. In some instances, a custody battle leads to parents throwing around abuse accusations for the sake of revenge. Nevertheless, incest is a real threat and a real crisis for many children. Don't dismiss your child's concerns when he or she says that your favorite uncle in the whole world makes your child sit on his lap far too long. Even if it's not abuse, you need to give your child permission to set his or her own body boundaries. And if it is abuse, you're better off facing the double tragedy of incest (which we'll review at length in chapters 6 and 12) sooner rather than later.

Abuse in Your Community

Child sex abuse affects communities. Every predator comes from someone's community. In fact, predators often play an important role in the community—beloved, respected, and trusted, perhaps for many years. So not only is the victim destroyed, but the community that loved and supported the abuser is betrayed and devastated. Friends may have been sworn to secrecy about the abuse. Others may have known about it, but perhaps they didn't know how to report or even if reporting was safe. In other cases, adults and child peers may have seen the victim with the perpetrator and failed to recognize the danger; they may have even condoned what they thought was a positive relationship.

The community often experiences both confusion and betrayal. A child who is carefully groomed—especially a teen—will support and defend an abuser, even while knowing that something terrible has been happening. For some victims, the abuse is tantamount to love, and to betray the abuser would be to betray the only person left in the victim's life. But peers don't understand this concept. As result, they too are left hurt, victimized by a predatory adult who may not have abused them, but who hoodwinked and exploited them to sexually molest other children.

Child sexual abuse acts like a nuclear bomb in a community: While not everyone is immediately injured, the effects and pain for everyone involved can last for decades.

No one teaches people how to react when someone they know is accused of abuse. The result? People react emotionally. Many times they side with the predator. Sometimes they even attack the victim. Either way, community reaction is seldom helpful.

The Survivors Network of those Abused by Priests (SNAP) addresses this issue head-on through an excellent handout that can help some communities. Although titled "What to Do When Your Priest Is Accused of Abuse,"[6] it can apply to abuse in any situation. Here are some of the relevant points, adapted for our discussion:

Be Open-Minded

It's human nature to recoil in horror when hearing about abuse. It's even natural to assume (and hope) that the allegations are false. Since child sex abuse is grossly underreported, however, it's more than likely that the allegations are true, even if they can't lead to an arrest due to the statute of limitations. Don't jump to conclusions or be quick to judge. Wait until you have all the information.

Allow Yourself to Feel Emotional

If someone you respect, admire, or love is accused of abuse, it's okay to feel hurt, angry, or betrayed. It's also healthy to allow those emotions to surface, so don't stuff them away. Just don't get carried away by emotions or do something drastic in the heat of the moment. In fact, if you think it will be helpful, go and talk to a professional who can help you try to sort through your feelings and respond in a healthy way.

Don't Try to Guess Who the Accuser Is

Crime victims are allowed to remain anonymous in the justice system. This is especially true for victims of sex abuse, who feel ashamed and isolated. Don't go on a witch hunt.

Understand That Abuse Victims Have Troubled Backgrounds

We know that predators target vulnerable and troubled children. As child sex abuse victims grow into adults, many suffer from addiction and anger issues. Criminal histories, depression, drug addiction, and mental illness are not uncommon. Don't judge a victim because they were horribly damaged by the abuse.

Don't Discredit a Victim Who Comes Forward Years Later

The survivors I have worked with seldom, if ever, came forward at the time of the abuse. Studies by the US Department of Justice and my own experience show that it takes many sex abuse victims decades to come forward, if they come forward at all.[7] That should not excuse a predator, who has more than likely spent the intervening years abusing other children.

Don't Allow Friends or Family to Make Disparaging Remarks about the Victim

Critical comments further victimize the abused and only discourage other victims from reaching out for help. Show compassion, and ask others in the community not to make hurtful comments. A six-year-old incest victim who is told that she's the "bad cousin" will only learn to be ashamed of her abuse. She will also (wrongly) blame herself for hurting the family by reporting a molesting grandfather.

If You Support the Accused, Do So Privately

If people in the community—other abused children, in particular—see that adults they love and respect are publicly supporting accused perpetrators, they will be less likely to report their own victimization. So if you really must stand behind the accused, do so privately.

Talk to Your Friends and Family about Abuse

Be frank. Encourage victims to come forward and get help—no matter who the abuser is.

Don't Be Blinded by Anger

Accusations of abuse lead to anger in the community, whether toward the perpetrator or the victim. Don't allow your anger to take over. Instead, channel your emotions into action or talk to a therapist. The rage you feel is valid, but acting on it is not.

* * *

I hope you are never in this situation, with a predator who tears your community apart by committing child sex abuse. But if you are affected by child sexual abuse, or if you know someone who is, therapists and support groups are available to help you through the crisis without causing additional pain to yourself, the victims, or the community. (See the Resources section near the end of this book.)

As a society, we have come to accept that church and community leaders are capable of committing terrible abuse. It is perhaps even more difficult to acknowledge that women and even our own family members can be predators. But there's no need to be paranoid. Just look out for the warning signs and follow your gut. Of all the people you know, 99.9 percent are not predators. The key is learning to protect yourself, your child, your family, and your community from the one-tenth of 1 percent who are.

Chapter 6

Institutions and Families: When Good People Do Bad Things

I would like to be able to tell you that institutions abhor abuse and immediately take action to stop child sexual abuse and put offenders behind bars. But we know that's not true. Sadly, the same is all too often true of the family unit, when family members simply cannot bring themselves to believe the victim's terrible story of abuse. Nothing tears an institution or a home apart more than when a child comes forward to report sexual abuse by a beloved member of that tight-knit group.

Are our institutions and families full of bad people? No. But even good people can do bad things.

What Is an Institution?

An institution is any group or organization that brings people of common interests together, asserts rules over people's behavior, or gives people jobs and financial reward. Some institutions do all three.

Examples of familiar institutions include churches, schools, community organizations, youth groups, universities, and even corporations.

A great way to think about institutions is like this: Anytime you wear or use the insignia or logo of a group with pride, that group is an institution.

Why Do We Love Institutions So Much?

Since the dawn of humankind, we have tried incessantly to do one thing: make sense of the world around us. We've created religion to help us make sense of the mysteries of God and the universe. We've created rules and laws to help us define behavior, morality, and worship. We've formed clans, tribes, cultures, cities, and civilizations to help us carve out our place in the world. We've created schools to educate our children. We've formed companies to provide goods and services.

These schools, churches, governments, and civic groups may have started with a single person, but they weren't long in growing larger and inviting more and more individuals to join them. Throughout time, these organizations have created their own brands, long before *brand* became a marketing buzzword. We associate churches with goodness and morality; schools with pride in achievement; companies with quality and care for workers; and civic groups with moral fiber and goodwill.

The brands stuck, even if the reality didn't match.

We love and trust our institutions so much that we hold them to a higher regard than people. Why? Because we believe that institutions can't hurt us like people can. It's a mistaken notion—institutions are run by people, of course—but that doesn't stop us from looking to long-standing organizations for stability and guidance.

Institutions give our lives meaning and structure. They give us a home in a chaotic world—roles, kinship, rules, and comfort. We rely on our institutions because they are bigger, stronger, and more stable than we are. Some have been around for centuries. They educate us, help us exercise our faith, offer lifelong friendships, and impart lessons we use our entire lives. Institutions are often the home of our best memories, our brightest moments, and they deliver solace in our times of greatest grief. We give some of them money—sometimes even directly from our paychecks—while others promise to *pay us* in return for years of service. Institutions host our favorite pastimes and entertainments, and provide identity, success, and community.

No wonder they often get a pass when it comes to child sexual abuse.

The Special Case of Religion

There is no institution that we hold more dearly and defend more fiercely than our church or spiritual home. Faith is the means by which the vast majority of people define themselves—even if that definition is "no religion."

Most of the time, religion provides people with a moral code and a way to worship that fills spiritual needs. But sometimes human foibles get in the way. Religion becomes an illusion—one that we refuse to surrender, because it is the supreme guiding factor in our lives. If we had to give it up, where else would we turn?

In the case of religion, our allegiance is strong and steadfast. But we have to remember that in the case of institutional religion, we are *not* talking about faith, God, or morality. We are talking about a human-made, human-operated institution.

While my abuse occurred from within the Catholic Church, you can substitute almost any church or religious organization's name and find the same thing happening. My abuse happened in an institution run by people. My abuse was *not* caused by the Catholic faith and is *not* a reflection on Catholics, their faith, or God. Victims who report abuse typically are not interested in taking down an entire institution.

Instead, we should see their stories as a wake-up call to how *people* act within religious organizations.

The case of Father Alejandro Castillo is a good example.

Castillo, a Southern California priest, was arrested in 2010 for sexually abusing a Riverside, California, boy. During the course of the investigation, three other boys came forward and said that Castillo had molested them as well.

As the allegations mounted, the police unearthed evidence that the local bishop probably knew the priest was a problem. It didn't look so good for Father Castillo. But this didn't deter churchgoers at Castillo's parish. They held car washes to raise money for his bail. They attended his court hearings en masse, holding signs to show their support. They told the media that the children were lying. No man at their church would ever hurt a child, they said. Their church fed the poor, helped immigrants get their legal documents, gave shelter to the homeless, and educated children. Their church, they said, would never allow a bad priest to preside over their parish.

But they were sorely wrong.

Eventually, Castillo pleaded guilty, acknowledging his guilt during his statement to the judge. All the car wash money raised to pay his bail was never returned to the financially strapped families. Castillo went to jail. When he was released, he was put on the sexual offender registry and, as a term of his parole, was not allowed to have contact with children.

But the parishioners did not lose their faith in Castillo. They simply could not believe that a priest and a man of the church could hurt a child. So, when Castillo was released, the parishioners threw him a "welcome home" party, complete with cake, balloons, and . . . children.

When the police learned about the party, Castillo was sent back to jail.

Why would good parents and loving families put their children at risk like this? Why would they alienate a victim's family and invite their children to a party celebrating an admitted child sex offender?

The general public was shocked. And why wouldn't they be? These impoverished, mostly Spanish-speaking families *knew logically* that Castillo had pleaded guilty. They knew that he had admitted his guilt. They knew he was on a strict parole. Yet they could not shed their blind faith in the institution that had defined their lives and their faith in God—even after the institution had let them down. In their view, to admit that Castillo was a child predator would undermine the foundation of their lives. In their view, Castillo *was* the church. They couldn't separate the institution and the man from God and their faith.

As a result, Castillo still has access to children—children whose parents are the former priest's biggest cheerleaders. Who loses? The kids.

Institutions versus Individuals

Due to their size, power, scale, reputation, influence, and goodwill, institutions almost always have the upper hand. Think about it: How many times have we said to ourselves at work, at school, or in another organization, "I am just one person. I can't make any real change." How many times have we seen whistleblowers destroyed? How many times have we watched as people who called out injustice were punished, ostracized, or alienated?

This kind of behavior thrived in the conformist and traditional 1950s and still is prevalent today among people who admire institutions or just don't want to "cause problems." We *want* to belong to a group, to be loved, and to earn the respect and companionship of our communities. When we speak out against our institutions, we put all of that at risk.

I remember once when I was a child, a car pulled over on the street where we lived. A man and a woman got out of the car and began screaming at each other. Screaming led to punches, and soon there was a full-fledged (and equally matched, mind you) fight in front of our home. When I went to my father and told him to call the police—like any dutiful child would—he put his hand on my shoulder and told me, "It's none of our business, sweetheart. We mustn't get involved." My mother agreed. Apparently, so did all the neighbors, who also heard the screams but did not call the police.

It didn't sit well with me.

These kinds of lessons followed me throughout my life. Anytime I saw injustice or issues, I was the first to raise my hand and demand change. In grade school, high school, and even college, well-meaning but misguided adults would tell me, "Don't cause problems. Just focus on your work." It was not a lesson I followed.

As I grew older and entered the business world, I saw firsthand how easy it is for people to justify inaction or wrong action if they believe they are doing it for a good cause. In the demise of a company like Enron, for example, the moral slide started with the "little things": overbilling for services, lying to clients, fudging income estimates, and throwing whistleblowing employees under the bus because it was "good for the company."

These moral slides are not unique to Enron. People keep corporate secrets, even when those secrets are bad, out of fear of losing jobs. Even when people do report things that are immoral or illegal, many consider their job done once they report up the chain of command. They don't follow through, demand action, or ensure that the complaint goes to the correct people. We all fall into that trap. We trust the institution to take care of it. We say, "I reported. It's out of my hands."

And the problems continue.

Enron traders did not go to work each day and say, "Gee, I am going to bankrupt a company and thousands of people." Joe Paterno didn't start his coaching speeches by saying, "Let's cover up everything we can about Jerry Sandusky." The leadership of the Boy Scouts didn't say,

"Let's set up a system so leaders who have been banned in one council can volunteer somewhere else, no questions asked." And I guarantee you that no one went into the priesthood because they wanted a career quietly "cleaning up" the messes caused by sex offenders. But otherwise good people can do seemingly abhorrent things if they think they are doing it for the institution or the "greater good."

An excellent example is Shattuck–St. Mary's, an elite boarding school in Faribault, Minnesota. The school produces so many top-ranked high school hockey players that it is locally known as a "feeder school" for the National Hockey League. Many of its other sports and academic programs are also highly ranked, and tuition as of 2014–2015 topped out at $45,000 a year. But in the late 1990s and early 2000s the school had a problem that still haunts them today.

Well-liked drama teacher Lynn Seibel was hosting "naked dance parties" in dormitory restrooms. He was also "teaching a class" of male students how to "enlarge their penis." Although school administrators had been hearing rumors for years—including outright statements from at least one student—they didn't call the police. Instead they decided to have a member of the board of directors "cold call" a number of the boys who were rumored to have taken part. The board member had no experience as an investigator and knew nothing about child sexual abuse.

In 2003, a school computer tech found child pornography on Seibel's school-owned computer. His excuse: that he had "accidentally" clicked on and downloaded images. Headmaster Nick Stoneman had a choice: He could call the police, insist on an investigation, and find potential victims (which would cause a temporary PR blow to the school), or he could quietly let the teacher go, which would keep any scandal under wraps.

Stoneman chose the latter option, paying Seibel $12,500 in exchange for a secrecy agreement. Seibel left the school and went to teach in Rhode Island. A few years later, Seibel moved to Hollywood to pursue his acting dreams. But after he appeared on the hit show

The Big Bang Theory as the "Naked Professor," Seibel's victims started reporting. In 2013, Seibel was convicted of molesting six students and sentenced to fifty-two months in prison.

Even after the sex abuse cover-up was exposed in a 2014 civil lawsuit against the school, school administrators stood behind their decision to pay Seibel and to hide the pornography and their suspicions from the police.

Stoneman—who is still the school's headmaster—had a choice. He chose the institution over the children in it. He was protecting what he thought was the "greater good," and Shattuck–St. Mary's students (and possible others) paid the price.

Charismatic Leaders

Institutions, by nature, encourage us to trust completely in the wisdom and power of their leadership, and many are built on a foundation of charismatic leaders. Think about the powerful preacher, the elected official, the football coach, the family patriarch, or the Boy Scout troop leader—individuals who rally crowds, unite people of differing opinions, energize people, and inspire movements. You know, the person of "movie star" stature who can get anyone to do anything. Usually, this kind of charismatic leader is untouchable. But when a charismatic leader is accused of abuse, it threatens not only the institution but the faith system that created the institution as well.

A charismatic leader does not have to be the head of the entire institution. Such leaders can exist at any level of an organization—as long as they are powerful and well-loved, and maintain a certain celebrity and status. They use their status to con children and families into believing they are trustworthy and above reproach. In fact, charismatic leaders do everything in their power to convince others that being the object of their attention makes a child special.

In June 2014, *Christianity Today*'s online Leadership Journal published a controversial article written by a youth minister who used his position to target and molest kids. The article, titled "My Easy Trip from Youth Minister to Felon: The Spiral into Sin That Destroyed My Life and Ministry,"[8] was later removed because the author continually referred to his crime as a consensual relationship and didn't disclose until the end of the article that the child was one of the youths in his care.

The piece is important for a couple of reasons: First, it shows how cunning predators seldom understand or consider the pain their crimes cause the victims. Just take a look at the title—the perpetrator fully admits that he destroyed his own life and ministry, but makes no mention of the victim. Second, it shows how a charismatic leader can use his or her position to commit child sex crimes. Here is an excerpt from the article.

> If I was applauded by the church, I was revered by the students . . . [If Christ] had shown up at one of my events, He would have been no higher than the second most important man there. I was the king of my own little kingdom . . .

When his wife found out that he was sexually abusing one of the kids in his youth group, she left him and took the children. The charismatic leader went to jail and lost everything.

The power of the charismatic leader cannot be underestimated in situations like this. When a willing audience sees the charismatic leader as a demigod, and that leader molests children, it destroys the victims, their families, and the community at large. For the community, the betrayal is deep: They have been exploited so a predator can get access to children. Many times, the community can't recover and the group breaks up permanently.

One of the best articles written on the subject of charismatic leaders and child sexual abuse is by author and twenty-five-year FBI veteran Joe Navarro. In his April 2014 piece in *Psychology Today*, "Why Predators Are Attracted to Careers in the Clergy,"[9] he outlines how institutions, including churches, provide predators a perfect place to molest children and remain protected. Following are some of the important points he makes:

- *Institutions give predators legitimacy.* A person with a high-ranking job in a church or school has a great deal of authority and power. Children are less likely to report abuse by powerful people, and powerful people are more likely to be protected by their colleagues and peers.

- *Institutions offer plenty of potential victims.* Institutions with children as members bring an endless supply of targets into contact with predators—often at a regular time and place.

- *Institutions have warning systems in place.* Colleagues and others within an institution can alert predators if their actions have been noticed. Institutions also have protections in place, like employee reviews, job transfers, and professional alliances, that can help a predator avoid being exposed.

- *Institutions can minimize negative publicity.* When an employee engages in criminal behavior, the last thing an institution wants to do is publicize that behavior with a public arrest or a media event that might bring out more survivors. Institutions tend to "handle" things in-house and are notoriously negligent when it comes to reporting abuse.

Institutions are a godsend to the predator. With protection and power, a predator can take the time to develop into a charismatic leader and hone the skills necessary to attract and groom children. Once they do attain the power and trust they seek, charismatic leaders can target abuse victims at will, often with the full force of the institution supporting them. But when we, as part of the community supporting these institutions, educate ourselves and understand that our children's safety should always be the top priority, we force our institutions to protect children rather than themselves.

Being Vigilant about Institutions

Institutions are a fact of life—and often a good fact of life. Our institutions help create order in our society, give us comfort, and provide us with friendship and community. No one wants to abolish them, but we must be vigilant when it comes to protecting children from institutional abuse.

Here are some questions to consider when examining the reputability of the institutions in your life:

- *Does the institution seem open and transparent?* When issues of any type arise, does the administration close ranks and remain secretive, or do they tell the membership about the problem and ask for help in making sure it never happens again?

- *Does the institution have a power structure that is not elected?* Do you have a say in the appointment of leadership? If you have a bad leader, does the membership have the power to fire him or her? If not, what other recourse do you have?

- *Is there "hero worship" in the institution?* Are there people in the organization who are "untouchable" or "superstars"?

- *Does the institution have a secret set of rules or secret files?* Does the institution have procedures or rituals that the general public cannot see? Does the institution keep secret personnel files about employees that contain criminal behavior?

- *Does the institution have a strong alumni or booster structure that donates large amounts of money?* Is the organization ever at risk of losing this money?

- *Has there been a covered-up scandal in the past?* Does the institution insist that all problems be handled internally? If so, is the same administration still in power? Or did the institution bring in new people at the very top, devoted to change and the safety of its members?

- *Is the institution considered an icon in the community?* Do leaders of the group get preferred and/or private access to community leaders or elected officials?

- *Does the institution discourage reporting or punish those who "tattle"?* Is whistleblowing considered a sin or crime against the institution? Have members who voiced opposition been ostracized, shut out, or punished?

Institutions and Cover-ups

Good people often do bad things for what they think are the right reasons, but there is never a right reason to cover up child sex abuse. Being vigilant about the institutions you welcome into your life includes doing whatever you can to ensure any abuse that occurs will not be covered up.

When you speak to people who are part of the institution, do you get the feeling they treasure the organization's reputation and the value it provides the community more than they value their members? This could be a warning sign that institution leadership (and even parents) may consider children's safety a "short-term cost." In other words, leadership may feel it's much easier to cover up the sexual abuse of a child and make the child "go away" than it is to face the risk of tarnishing the institution's reputation.

Remember, when there are secrets, there is cover-up. If you are going to require your toddler to follow the "no secrets" rule (see chapter 10), you should demand the same transparency and accountability from the institutions where you spend your time and your money, and where you send your child.

If you are a part of a congregation with little to no power over the selection of your leader, pay special heed. If you do not get any say in hiring this person, you cannot be assured of his or her past or trustworthiness. Plus, if members have no control in this person's job, he or she may hold special power in the community. Should abuse happen, these conditions make an institution ripe for cover-up. Take heed, use caution, and always put your child first.

Reporting Abuse in an Institution

If you see or suspect abuse in an institution, report it first to law enforcement. *Then* report to the institution. Why? You do not want to give the institution a chance to minimize your report, hide the abuse, do an "internal investigation," or give the abuser a "heads-up."

Chances are, the institution will want to do the right thing. But the impulse to hide the problem can be powerful. Don't open an opportunity for cover-up. Schools, churches, community groups, and other such organizations are not in the sex abuse investigation business. Law enforcement is. Let law enforcement do its job.

Reporting suspected or seen abuse is the *best* way to show your institution and fellow members that you love them, respect them, and want to protect the children in their care.

How to Protect Your Child from Institutional Abuse

When it comes to protecting your child from institutional sex abuse, you have to ask the right questions. To do this, you have to be strong. You are not only scrutinizing individuals, but also asking questions that will ruffle feathers and threaten people who are used to the "status quo"—or worse, secrecy.

Here are some steps you can take to make sure your child is not involved in an institution that puts him or her at increased risk.

Ask about Background Checks

Ask about hiring practices, background checks, and past allegations. Most institutions that deal with children do background checks, but many do not check higher-ups. This should go without saying, but it still needs to be made clear: Avoid institutions with convicted criminals among their leadership. If a high-ranking person has been convicted of a crime, consider placing your trust in a different organization. For example, in 2012, Kansas City–St. Joseph Diocese's Bishop Robert Finn was convicted of child endangerment. He was allowed to remain a bishop for three more years, even though he could not pass his own background checks. It wasn't until April 2015, three years after Finn's conviction, that he resigned. Finn is still a powerful bishop, but no longer heads a diocese.

Do Your Own Research

If you have heard about allegations of abuse, lawsuits, or settlements, do your research. It's not easy for victims to come forward, and in all of my experience, I have never personally dealt with a frivolous lawsuit. In fact, I have dealt with hundreds of victims who, because of the statute of limitations, were not able to expose their offender, though often that person was still working with children. Civil lawsuits are not frivolous. No one wants to go through that process unless they truly suffered abuse at the hands of a predator.

The civil justice system is not easy. Victims must carry a huge burden of proof. Lawyers for the offenders and institutions often launch full-scale attacks on the victim's credibility and integrity. Victims endure this process because justice and accountability are worth it. Exposing predators, abuse, and cover-up is the goal, especially for victims who have been forced to remain silent for years. The ultimate goal is to warn the community and parents . . . parents like you. If your church or your child's school has been sued for abuse by numerous victims, there is clearly a problem within that institution. Consider a new school or church.

Demand a Higher Standard

If the leadership of the institution downplays past allegations or lawsuits, calling them "stale," "decades old," or "in the past," consider a new group, especially in the case of a church. Why? A religion's mission is to help those in pain, not minimize the pain of victims. If a group is willing to minimize a victim who already met the burden of proof in court, I can guarantee you that they will minimize the pain of the next child who is abused.

Demand Accountability

Demand a voice, accountability, and transparency in how children are cared for in the institution. That includes a say in who is given access to your child.

Ask about the Reporting Procedure

If an employee or volunteer who sees or suspects abuse is told to report it to a supervisor instead of to police, demand that the rule be changed. All people working with children should be required to report to the authorities first. Police, not friends and colleagues of the accused, must be allowed to investigate a crime. Every member of the institution's leadership should have the phone numbers to report abuse, including the Childhelp hotline. If the organization's procedure is to do an internal investigation before contacting the police about abuse, consider choosing another organization.

Listen to the Grapevine

I am not encouraging you to spread rumors, but if there is a suspicion of abuse or inappropriate behavior, report it. Also, observe how whistleblowers are treated in the organization. If people who report problems of any type have been ostracized, ask why. If there have been any allegations of misconduct, ask that organization leadership openly and publicly disclose what has happened.

Believe the Victim

Understand that false allegations do occur. But also understand that child sex abuse is grossly underreported. It is far more likely that abuse is unreported than that an allegation is false. If abuse has already been reported, accept the victim's story—it wasn't easy for him or her to share. If a child has told you about abuse, report the crime. Believe the child.

The Family: Our First and Foremost Institution

Nowhere else is the "greater good" more important than in the family unit. Our family is our foundation; it is how we define ourselves from birth. We are someone's son or daughter. We may be someone's brother or sister. We may grow to become someone's parent. We chart our genealogies. For as far back as there have been people, our families have defined us, protected us, and given us meaning and roles to fulfill. The family is our first institution.

Just as in the community at large, allegations of incest within the family institution are the equivalent of a nuclear bomb. Everyone is affected, everything is damaged, and the fallout lasts a lifetime. Nothing can prepare a family for the moment when someone makes allegations of incest. And since family members are usually never prepared, they respond with knee-jerk reactions. All too often family members rally around the accused, even if they have real cause to believe that the alleged victim is telling the truth.

Many times, family members simply cannot believe that someone they love so much could do something so terrible. Many victims are suffering from emotional issues, including addiction, depression, or rage—often caused or made worse by the abuse—leaving family members in doubt about the truth of the victim's account. Another sad reason that families rally around the abuser involves the "standard of living" defense. These are cases where family members (usually wives) realize that if they believe the victim, they run the risk of losing their comfortable standard of living. For example, if Dad is accused of abuse and ends up going to jail, Mom believes that she and the children run the risk of losing their home, savings, and standing in the community.

All of these cases are tragic. Perhaps most tragic of all, however, is when family members know the truth but love the perpetrator so much that they simply do not care.

The next step for family members who decide to support the abuser is, even more tragically, to discredit and alienate the victim and anyone else who sides with the child. This happens especially when the victim is a young child. Children—especially older children—know or sense that saying they were sexually abused by a family member is likely to tear the family apart, so they are unlikely to report.

As great as the fear is of outing someone loved by the entire family, reporting abuse by a parent is even more frightening. Many times, the child won't report out of fear that the abusing parent will go to jail and the family will lose their home and financial support. If the family member is respected and admired (and not the "black sheep" or a convicted felon already), the child fears the backlash for telling the truth.

Beyond ostracizing, some family members may even threaten the child and anyone who believes him or her. The accusers might be told to keep things under wraps in order to protect the family or the abuser's reputation. It's also quite common for the victim to be told that he or she brings shame to the family. And other children in the family will often bully or berate the child, parroting what they hear older family members say in public or private.

Often, the child victim will remain quiet. But sometimes, when a victim grows into adulthood and learns that the perpetrator is targeting a younger child, the older victim will finally come forward and report in order to protect the younger child. Most of the time, however, in the battle of family institution versus child, the child barely stands a chance.

How to Help a Victim of Incest

We don't get to choose our families. But in cases of incest, we do have the choice and the obligation to report.

Report Incest

If your child tells you he or she has been abused by a family member, report it to the police or the Childhelp National Child Abuse Hotline (800-4-A-CHILD). If you see a child in your family being shunned or shamed for reporting abuse, do something about it. Step in and care for the child. Support the victim. Help the victim create a new and supportive space.

Walk Away

If you are supporting a child who is a victim of incest, and you and the child are being hurt or shunned by the family, walk away. This may be one of the hardest things you do, but it's far easier than inflicting further pain on the child. Demand that the situation be open and discussed—not a family secret, which only further shames the child into silence and believing that the abuse was his or her fault.

The most important thing is to get the victim far away from the perpetrator and his or her defenders. You are not likely to change the mind of the abuser's supporters, but you can help the victim create a new family full of love.

Chapter 7

Child Pornography:
Images of Child Abuse

No one likes to think about child pornography. In fact, we dislike thinking about it so much that we trivialize it in a way that allows the child pornography market to expand at an exponential rate.

Best-selling crime novelist John Grisham got himself into hot water in a 2014 interview in the *London Telegraph*,[10] saying that men who look at pornographic images of teenage girls should not serve long jail times. He portrayed looking at these images of child abuse as an innocent habit and lamented that one of his friends had served a three-year jail sentence for possession of child pornography. Grisham minimized the abuse by saying that his friend foolishly clicked on a computer link and then accidentally downloaded images—the same excuse offered by boarding school drama teacher Lynn Seibel.

This chapter explains why Grisham's view is so dangerous.

What Is Child Pornography?

The definition of child pornography includes photos, computer-generated images, and videos of a child in a sex act. It also includes photos of a child where the focus of the image is on the child's genitalia. The sex act can be with an adult, another child, or alone. In any of these types of images, a child is being sexually abused and exploited. The images are created, traded, bought, and sold through complex underground trafficking systems, including darknets (Internet servers that cannot be traced), or are transferred using key drives or other means.

Child pornography is a federal crime with huge consequences, both for possession of such images and for aiding or facilitating their sale or transfer. There is no "age of consent" variation; as far as the federal government is concerned, it's child pornography if the person in the photos is under the age of eighteen. This is serious stuff, and the federal government comes down hard on violators: First-time offenders receive minimum sentences of five to thirty years, with the sentence going up if the images were transported (digitally or otherwise) over state lines.

There is a reason that lawmakers and judges come down hard on people who view child pornography: Child pornography is the abuse and exploitation of children at its worst. The images are disgusting and show children being forced to do horrible things. These children were abused and photographed for the sexual pleasure of thousands of predatory adults. Simply viewing child pornography constitutes sexual abuse of the child in the photo. By creating a demand for these images, those who view them are ensuring that sexual predators continue abusing children. Viewing child pornography is criminal behavior that must be immediately reported.

We minimize child pornography by calling it names like "kiddie porn" when in fact these are images of children being sexually abused or engaging in abusive sex acts. We trivialize it by saying that it's a "victimless crime" or that it's perfectly natural for men to be aroused by "well-developed" teens. And with the rise of the Internet, creating, storing, and sharing child pornography has become easier than ever.

Numerous cases across the country continue to reveal the damage child pornography causes and reinforce the importance of addressing this issue directly in any discussion of child sex abuse. For a child who is sexually abused, the damage can last a lifetime. If that child is photographed or videoed while being abused, the abuse and its digital trail can even outlast the victim's lifetime.

The vast majority of people who create and view child pornography are men. Not all of them will go on to abuse children. But because the person viewing is sexually aroused by children, there is a *huge* risk that this person will go on to offend. If you see or suspect child pornography, call 911 immediately.

The Myth of the "Victimless Crime"

Some people claim that child pornography is a "harmless habit." Even people who should know better—religious leaders, community and elected officials, law enforcement officials—have claimed that child pornography is a victimless crime because the person looking at it is not actually touching or physically harming a child.

Nothing could be further from the truth.

Let's take a look at how these abusive images are made. Many are produced by adults who are actively sexually abusing the children in the images. The predator may or may not be in the photographs or videos, but you can be sure that behind the scenes he or she is using grooming techniques, threats, drugs, alcohol, or violence to force the child into public performance of a sex act. No child wants to be in damaging, humiliating images or wants to engage in the acts forced on them. Sometimes the producers go even further and force children to engage in sex acts with other children. This forces the children into a mutual silence built on shame and secrecy.

Once the pornography is created, the child is even more vulnerable. To keep the child compliant, all the abuser or producer has to do is threaten to send the photos or videos to the child's family, friends, or church—or release them on social media. The result? The child is trapped in abuse and shame even longer than a child who is not caught on camera.

Here is something else to remember: These images are in no way "innocent." Abusive photos cannot be "mistaken" for innocent ones. They often portray beatings, violence, imprisonment, force, rape, or sodomy, or they are pictures obviously focused on the child's genitals. They are gross and they are nasty. And for the victims—kids forced to participate—it's devastating and damaging.

Where Do the Kids Come From?

Sometimes the children seen in these abusive images are unknowing victims of carefully placed cameras. Pornographers have positioned cameras in children's bathroom stalls, bedrooms, and other places in order to get pictures of genitalia. In other cases, the photos are taken of little girls under their skirts, boys changing in locker rooms, or at pools or the beach.

Other children seen in pornographic images are crime victims who are being exploited and sold for sex, otherwise known as "sex trafficking." They may be runaways who have been groomed by pimps and sold to men on a nightly basis. They may be children who are already being abused by a family member, close family friend, teacher, or community leader. These are kids who have already been carefully groomed for abuse and then forced that extra step further into being photographed. Other victims are coerced, knowingly or unknowingly, by drugs and alcohol.

The victims are not bad or immoral; they are just kids. "Good" kids and kids from "good" homes have been forced into child pornography, as have at-risk kids and kids from broken homes or group homes. It can happen to any child.

What about Older Kids?

Despite John Grisham's remarks about his friend, there is nothing accidental or innocent about finding and downloading these kinds of images, regardless of the child's age. First of all, child pornography lives on the Internet, but not on the Internet that you and I surf every day. Child porn is found on "darknets"—highly protected, private, encrypted peer-to-peer connections. If you are a part of this type of "community," you know where to look. Otherwise, it is difficult to "innocently" stumble across this kind of material.

Second, the pictures that John Grisham's friend downloaded were bad enough to be easily traced. The Canadian police came knocking soon after Grisham's friend accessed the images. If the images were bad enough for the police to come in, arrest him, and successfully convict him, there was nothing "innocent" about those images.

Third, by drawing a line at teenage girls, Grisham and his friend minimized the pain these children endured. They tried to remove the immoral and criminal aspect of the crime. By rationalizing that these were female teenagers instead of young boys, Grisham and his friend supported the mistaken idea of child pornography as harmless and somehow acceptable, as long as the children are of a certain age and gender. But if those pictured are under eighteen years old, then in the eyes of the law, of society, and of their parents—and most likely in their own eyes, too—they are children. A sixteen-year-old girl who is trafficked for sex is just as hurt and damaged as a ten-year-old boy would be.

Grisham claimed to have no idea that the kids in these photos were victims of crime, violence, and sexual abuse. But after the immediate uproar his interview caused, he knows it now.

Pornography or No?

What if you aren't sure whether or not something is child pornography? The phrase "I know it when I see it"—which became famous when a US Supreme Court justice used it to describe the threshold for whether or not a film was obscene—works just as well for images of child abuse. If you see or hear about a photograph or video that makes you wonder whether it's child pornography, you can bet it is.

If you see child pornography or suspect it, call the police. If you suspect that it may be on computers in your home, call the police. If you suspect that someone is taking pornographic pictures or videos of children, call the police. It is not your job to be an investigator or a detective. The police vigorously investigate these kinds of allegations, so you need not worry that the cops will drop the ball. Remember, if it's stored on a computer you own, you are in possession of child pornography, which is a state and federal crime. It is your moral obligation to report this to the police. Believe me, things will go much worse for you if you *don't* report it.

A Moral Obligation to Report

If you know about child pornography and don't do anything, you can get in trouble.

If you live in a state that considers you a mandated reporter, yes. (See chapter 8 for a longer discussion of mandatory reporting.) But let's look at your moral obligation: If you know that someone is producing or selling child pornography, you are a witness to horrific child abuse. You owe it to yourself and to the children in those images to report.

Here's a story that can shed some light on the role of mandated reporters. A Catholic priest in Kansas City was producing and in possession of thousands of images of child pornography, mostly images of the genitals of young girls. When the local bishop, Robert Finn, found out, he sent the priest to live in a convent, where he continued to take more lewd photos of children. The priest, Father Shawn Ratigan, went on to begin serving a fifty-year prison sentence for the production and possession of child pornography. Finn, who didn't report the pornography or the threat to the police, was later found guilty of one count of failure to report child sexual abuse.

Finn knew and didn't report; now he has a record. Many believe he has morally failed the Catholics in his diocese. He claimed it was little more than ignorance. But since you are reading this book, you have the tools and knowledge to report. So do it!

The Trouble with "Sexting"

Before camera phones and the Internet, teens seldom (if ever) took nude or seminude self-portraits and gave them to their boyfriends or girlfriends. It was way too risky: The local drug store wouldn't develop the photos and were required to call parents and the police. The advent of Polaroid instant film made taking and sharing photos easier, but the average teenager rarely used the process to share nude images.

Enter the Internet. Now, with the push of a button or the swipe of a touchscreen, teens can take naked self-portraits or create lewd videos and send them to anyone, anywhere. It's easy. Far too easy.

Is "sexting" child pornography? Technically, yes. If the photo or video is of the teen engaged in a sex act (alone or with others) or is focused on the genitalia, it is child pornography. Are the feds going to prosecute same-age, minor teens for willingly taking, sending, and receiving these photos? Probably not. *But that does not mean the images will never end up on child pornography darknets or websites.*

While your daughter may think that her current boyfriend would never do anything with those naked photos and videos, all it takes is one broken heart or one angry reaction for the boy to send the photos around the world. And no matter how much your teen trusts her boyfriend, phones are hacked, stolen, and "borrowed" all the time. Any photo can become a public photo. Just consider the slew of celebrity nude photos that have been hacked, stolen, and shared around the world. While the scandal may be helpful to some celebrities' careers, publicized nude photos can destroy your teen's reputation, chances at college, or even future jobs.

Chapter 13 addresses the issue of sexting in more detail. But this is what I tell teens who think taking and sending nude photos is "sexy": *Only take photos and videos of yourself that you would be willing to share with your parents and grandparents.* Because if you take nude photos of yourself and send them over the Internet—and they get into the wrong hands—your privacy and body are no longer yours.

Your child has only one shot at innocence. A single nude photo can take that all away. The more we can show our teens that *nothing* sent over the Internet is private, the more we can protect them from the shame and embarrassment of being "exposed" . . . and from the grips of a predator.

Chapter 8

What If You Suspect Abuse? Mandatory Reporting

You may be someone who bought this book because you had a "sinking feeling." Maybe you know of a situation in your community that makes you feel a little "hinky." Perhaps there is a child at your church or other organization who is showing signs of sexual abuse. Maybe someone has disclosed to you that he or she is a victim of child sexual abuse.

Many of us have experienced one or more of these situations in some form, but few of us know what to do. Unfortunately, when it comes to issues like sexual abuse, it's too easy to do nothing, because it feels *safer*. We are scared about getting involved. We fear that we might cause trouble or ruin someone's reputation. Or we hope that a "mandated reporter" will do the reporting for us.

From a moral standpoint, however, *we are all mandated reporters*.

Later chapters in this book will discuss how to help children share with their parents what they see and experience. We will also discuss how to help our children feel safe enough to tell us about abuse they experience, witness, hear about, or suspect. But before we can impart this insight to our children, we must take it to heart ourselves. That's why you need to think of *yourself* as a mandated reporter.

If a child is being abused, you may be the only person who can stop it.

What Is a Mandated Reporter?

Regrettably, there are no hard-and-fast national rules about who is a mandated reporter. Even at state and local levels, there is little consequence for a mandated reporter who does not report. Law enforcement does not have a great deal of time to press charges against mandated reporters who fail to report child sexual abuse, and the cases seldom go to trial even if charges are pressed.

Some states such as Delaware, Indiana, and Mississippi share my view and consider all adults mandated reporters. But no one wants to punish the average citizen who suspected abuse and didn't know how to report. That's why other states have set up special classes of workers who are mandated reporters under the law and are subject to penalty if they do not report suspected or witnessed abuse. Most of these mandated reporters are people who work directly with children, including teachers, school administrators, day care providers, medical professionals, therapists, doctors, clergy, and first responders (those who are first on the scene in times of crisis). These people are usually outside the family structure and can observe the child and the child's signs and symptoms objectively.

Many times, a parent first learns that his or her child may be a victim of abuse from a mandated reporter. Pediatricians are expertly trained to examine a child and determine whether there are signs of abuse. School therapists and elementary school teachers are often the first to hear about problems in a child's home. Early childhood educators and day care workers know what is healthy play and what isn't. Some also change diapers and can see visible signs of abuse. That's why lawmakers decided these professionals should be required to report—and why workplaces ask them to submit to criminal background checks.

A Brief History of Mandatory Reporting

Anyone who is familiar with novels like *Oliver Twist* or who understands the history of child labor knows that child protection is a relatively new concept, only gaining a foothold in the United States in the late nineteenth century. While many US states had a Society for the Prevention of Cruelty to Children by 1900, the installation of mandatory reporting of witnessed or suspected crimes took another sixty years.

The Journal for the American Medical Association's landmark article "The Battered Child Syndrome," published in 1962, brought with it a sea change. Written by Denver physician Dr. C. Henry Kempe and his colleagues, the article marked the first time that the diagnosis, treatment, and symptoms of child abuse and child sexual abuse were treated as academic subjects. As a result of the dramatic findings and widespread publicity, less than five years later more than forty state legislatures had implemented laws requiring mandatory reporting of abuse. Now, every US state has some kind of mandatory reporting law.

To view the mandatory reporting laws in your state, visit the US Child Welfare Information Gateway at Childwelfare.gov.

Why Is Mandatory Reporting Important?

Before the advent of mandatory reporting, hundreds of thousands of child abuse and child sex abuse victims fell through the cracks of the system. Physicians, teachers, and others who worked directly with children were reticent to report what they saw or knew because of fears of retribution or intruding in other people's privacy.

The early to mid-twentieth century was also an era of "spare the rod, spoil the child." Many parents and "experts" in the fields of parenting and education felt that serious physical punishments—including beatings that left cuts and bruises—were effective and positive ways to enforce discipline. A child showing up in a doctor's office with bruises in 1940 may have simply neglected to do his chores, and family doctors did not want to intrude on what they saw as a family's "discipline style."

The current proliferation of news stories about child sexual abuse started only because victims began speaking out in the past few decades. It's been a victim-driven movement—adults who were sexually abused as children demanded that their stories be told. As time passed and more victims were able to prove that yes, their accounts were true and accurate, the media was more inclined to give these stories a chance. Hearing about sexual abuse was no longer something that repulsed and repelled people. The media got a positive response, and the public showed righteous outrage. These stories became tales of justice and redemption for victims who demanded that the perpetrators be put behind bars.

Even after victims began to tell their stories, societal views on sex and abuse continued to evolve. For example, only in the past ten years or so has society acknowledged that boys can be sexually victimized by adult women. Even so, the myth that older women help "break in" boys sexually still prevails. A rash of arrests started up in the mid-2010s, however, of female teachers who were accused of molesting male and female students. A great example is the case of two teachers from Southern California who were arrested in 2015 on charges that they hosted an "alcohol and sex party" for male students on the beach in San Clemente, a small community in southern Orange County. As recently as ten years ago, the police may have been inclined to look the other way, citing the old "boys will be boys" mentality and releasing the teachers with little more than a wink. But because of our greater awareness that any adult in a position of power who is sexual with a child is committing a crime, more and more women are being rightfully punished for sexually abusing children.

Mandatory reporting laws gave doctors, teachers, cops, and other people who work with children permission—and the state's blessing—to report what they suspected. Because these caregivers were able to tell an investigating agency about their suspicions, it was no longer the duty of the doctor or the teacher or the school principal to investigate claims, interview victims, or make conclusions. More important, if a mandated reporter was wrong, he or she was not liable for making the complaint (unless it was intentionally false and malicious).

Why Can't We Always Rely on Mandated Reporters?

It would be so easy if we could sit back and know that every mandated reporter was going to report every case of child sexual abuse out there. But we know that isn't true or even remotely possible.

There are thousands of children who are being sexually abused right now who will never catch the eye or suspicion of a mandated reporter. The child may not be in school, may not get regular medical care, or may not show any of the signs and symptoms of abuse when in the care of mandated reporters. No mandated reporter can monitor every child he or she passes in the street.

But there are also more pernicious and ultimately tragic reasons that mandated reporters may overlook these incidents, including neglect of duty or refusal to follow the law. Mandated reporters are human and subject to all the foibles and flaws that affect the rest of us. They give cunning abusers the benefit of the doubt, question children's stories, or even question their own sanity when considering a case. They may weigh the abuse against problems in the foster care system and assume that the child is better off at home than living with strangers. Some probably hope the abuse will stop on its own and the child will "make it through."

The system isn't perfect. Even when mandated reporters *do* report and investigators believe that abuse occurred, a lack of evidence or a family unwilling to press charges can stymie an arrest or stop a prosecution in its tracks. Media stories continually remind us that simply because a state's social services system is involved, a child is not always protected. It's a sad truth.

Lack of Training

Many mandated reporters are not properly trained. Even if they are trained, the training might not be updated, refreshed, or enforced. While many state and local governments do their best to make sure that training materials, courses, and even online classes on reporting are available, many mandated reporters simply do not receive the training, for a number of reasons: work overload, oversight, budget cuts, staffing shortfalls, lack of access, ignorance of the laws.

If you are or believe you may be a mandated reporter, visit your state's social services website to search for mandated reporter trainings that are available to you and your colleagues free of charge. The general public is also allowed to take these courses, which are seldom longer than a couple of hours.

Human Mistake

While the vast majority of mandated reporters consider child welfare their first priority, many civil and criminal cases across the country have shown that far too often, mandated reporters put other priorities first—especially if reporting the abuse will hurt or threaten an institution, school, or organization.

Unfortunately, the criminal statute for failure to report is quite short: Prosecutors usually have less than three years to find out that a mandated reporter didn't report abuse. As a result, we usually learn about a reporter's failure when victims come forward in civil lawsuits. In my own case, numerous school and church officials knew in 1987 that the man who had molested me had also molested at least one other girl. But when I gained access to secret school and church documents after my case settled in 2005, documents showed that no one at the school reported the abuse to Child Protective Services. Was this malicious? Did these administrators want to intentionally hurt me? No. They gave a predator the benefit of the doubt and wanted to quash any hint of scandal. They were human, and they made a grave mistake.

This kind of behavior is certainly not unique to my case. In 2012, the Boy Scouts of America turned over more than 1,900 of their "perversion files," which showed a systematic and dangerous cover-up of abuse. In 99 percent of the cases, mandated reporters did not turn over what they knew to police. Maybe they didn't understand the law. Maybe they thought that kicking predators out of Scout troops would solve the problem. But they were wrong. And kids were put directly at risk.

Regrettably, therapists have fallen into this same trap. In a 2012 criminal trial of Sacramento, California, area foster and respite home operator and pastor Tommy Gene Daniels, a therapist testified that she continued to send children to live with the pastor even though she knew his licenses to run care homes had been revoked. When a child reported abuse to the therapist, she testified that she conducted an "internal investigation" with Daniels's wife. She never reported the abuse to authorities and later admitted that she had a business relationship with the now-convicted molester. As a mandated reported, she made a poor judgment: It wasn't her job to investigate. It was her job to report.

Other reasons reporters don't call authorities are less nefarious but just as reckless. Some claim a fear of retribution from their supervisors, the accused, or the parents of the child. Others claim they did not believe the child's report. Still other cases involved a misunderstanding of the signs and symptoms of abuse, or the hope that someone else would make the call. Sometimes, when a victim discloses that a celebrity, a cleric, or a prominent member of the community is an abuser, the mandated reporter does not disclose out of fear that a false allegation will ruin the life and career of the victim, the accused, *and* the reporter.

The two most common anecdotal reasons that mandated reporters do not report what they know are 1) when the victim begs the reporter to "keep the secret," and 2) when a reporter feels that the privacy of a family is more important than the safety of a child. When a victim of sexual abuse discloses and is sad, scared, and begging for trust, it is tempting for anyone, including a mandated reporter, to keep the secret. Unfortunately, this only perpetuates the cycle of abuse.

Institutional Allegiance

Many mandated reporters do not report because of their allegiance to their employer or to the institution where the offender works. The Sandusky scandal at Penn State University and cases of sexual abuse cover-up in the Boy Scouts and the Catholic Church are prime examples. When an institution is admired more than the children in its care are prized, mandated reporters are less likely to report out of fear of hurting the institution's reputation. Many institutions, such as religious organizations, require high-ranking officials to take oaths of allegiance to the organization. When allegations are made, mandated reporters are more likely to go to a supervisor for permission to report, to conduct an internal investigation, or to simply claim the allegation is false rather than take the risk of subjecting the institution to police or media scrutiny.

Still the Best System We Have

Yes, there are some problems with the mandatory reporting system. But it is far better than any system we have had in the past. Anytime that anyone is trained to spot and report abuse, children are safer. The key is to continue spreading the word, insist that more adults get trained in how to report, and empower "regular folks" (that's you and me) to spot suspected abuse and report it.

What If Someone Tells You He or She Has Been Abused?

Learning about or suspecting child sexual abuse can bring with it a great deal of confusion, fear, and other emotions for both you and the victim. Here are some guidelines for what to do when the victim finally opens up to his or her chosen confidant: you.

Tell the Person You Believe Him or Her

Disclosing abuse takes a great deal of trust, something that many victims don't have. If a victim discloses to you, that means that he or she trusts you and is hoping (consciously or unconsciously) that you will do the right thing. If you react with fear, disbelief, disgust, or skepticism, you may silence the victim for years to come.

Reassure the Victim That the Abuse Was Not His or Her Fault

No child deserves to be abused, and no child "asks" for it. But because children are egocentric, they instinctively blame themselves. Plus, since most child victims are carefully groomed, the child will be loyal to and even love his or her abuser. Telling the child that abuse is a crime and was not his or her fault is very important.

Tell the Victim That You Will Help

If the victim is a child, teen, or young adult, explain that because you care about him or her, you need to report what you have learned to the police. The child may be scared, but offer reassurance that you will support him or her and that by talking to the police, together you can help keep other children safe.

If the victim is an adult, explain that you will help him or her report the crimes. Tell the victim that it is likely the abuser is still "out there," hurting children. Assure the victim that he or she can protect children at risk right now by reporting the abuse. Explain that the victim may still have civil and criminal rights to expose the abuse, and encourage him or her to take action as soon as possible—but only if and when the person is ready.

Tell the victim that you are available and willing to listen to whatever he or she is willing to disclose. Explain that it's natural to be scared, angry, or depressed. Reassure the victim that you will be there for whatever help and support he or she needs. You can also recommend professional support and support groups in your area and, if you are able, offer to help with research. Support groups are a tremendous resource and have helped millions of victims heal. These groups have also led the charge to change state legislation, increase victims' rights, and put offenders behind bars. You can find more resources and a thorough list of national support groups and victims' advocacy organizations on my website, Casteix.com.

Follow These Reporting Guidelines

When preparing to report child sexual abuse, remember the most important thing: You are doing what is necessary to help the victim escape a horrific, damaging situation and get his or her life on the right track. What you are doing is brave and important. Do not undervalue it or take it lightly.

Here are some guidelines to follow.

What to Do If You or a Child Is a Victim

If your child has been sexually abused, you witness child sex abuse, you are a victim of sexual assault, or you discover someone is in immediate danger, *dial 911 right now.* If your child or another child tells you he or she has been abused, report it as soon as possible. The same goes if you have been raped or are a victim of sexual assault. Dial 911 immediately, and retain all clothing and other evidence you can. If there are bruises, scrapes, or marks, take pictures if the victim will allow you. Administer first aid if necessary, and ensure that the victim does not go into shock.

What to Do If You Suspect Child Sexual Abuse

This is where many people decide that doing nothing is safer than taking action. Suspicions are scary things. We second-guess ourselves. We assume that the child's parents have it under control. We think that the child is just going through a phase. And yes, sometimes these things can be true.

But what if they are not? What if you are in the middle of a worst-case scenario? What if your suspicions are not just a confused conclusion by a concerned neighbor? No one is suggesting a witch hunt. In fact, I am encouraging you to do the opposite: Come into a situation well-informed and with the ability to take positive action. Chapter 1 outlines many of the signs and symptoms of child sexual abuse. These are not set in stone, but your gut can be a good guide for you. If your gut says, "I think I need to take the next step," do it.

Don't worry: Reporting suspected child sex abuse will *not* bring the SWAT team to the child's home. Police detectives and news vans will not circle your home. In fact, the reporting authorities already know that you are probably scared and reticent to make the call. That is why there are hotlines with trained operators who can ask you questions, help you figure out what you saw and/or suspect, and show you the appropriate next steps (or take over the next steps themselves).

Call the Childhelp National Child Abuse Hotline at 800-4-A-CHILD. (Also, the Childhelp.org website is well worth your review now, before you encounter a situation where you need immediate answers.) When you call the hotline, a trained crisis operator will talk to you about what you saw, what you suspect, and the next steps you should take. He or she will carefully walk you through the entire process.

If you suspect that a child who is not your child is being abused, and the parents are not the suspected abusers, talk to the parents. If you think that the parents will not take action and the child is in danger, call Childhelp. The trained operator will help you assess your suspicions and alert you to the next steps you should take.

If the victim of sexual assault is an adult, call the Rape, Abuse, and Incest National Network (RAINN) at 800-656-HOPE. They can help guide you through the reporting process and help the victim get immediate medical and therapeutic care.

Part Three

The Protected Child

Chapter 9

Preparations: Loving and Protecting Your Baby

Adult victims of child sex abuse have huge obstacles to overcome when they have their own children. Survivors have to address the irrational fear in their own lives and understand that what happened to them—like what happened to me—does not have to happen to their own child.

You don't have to be a survivor of abuse to experience fears about protecting your new baby. All parents have fears. Fortunately, you also have the tools below.

The First Few Months

When I had my own son, I was initially wracked with the same fears you may have. I became one of those panicky parents who sees goblins behind every closed door and believes that the world is full of bad people who want to hurt my child. Most terrifying was the concern that I wouldn't be a good mother—so how could I possibly defend a child against a big, mean world?

Slowly but surely, I calmed down. I looked back at my own child-hood experience and at the experiences of the hundreds of victims I knew. I managed to find the positive aspect beneath all the fear: I deeply understood that I was my baby's first and best defense in life. I had a job to do, and I was going to do it to the best of my ability. The only way I could protect my baby was to empower myself and empower this child to give me signals if there was something wrong.

Am I a perfect parent? Heck, no. But my goals were simple: I wanted to raise a child who was safer from abuse and whom people *liked to be around*. What kind of child is that? A happy, self-confident child. A compassionate kid. A child who likes to laugh and have fun, a child who understands patterns, boundaries, safety, and who is not surrounded by trauma or chaos. I have no expectations that my child will become the president of the United States or a Nobel laureate. But if my son can wake up in the morning and like who he is, have self-control, and be empowered and someone whom people like to be around, then he is a success.

He also needed to be well-armored. But how do you arm an infant against abuse and other dangers? It's much easier than you think.

The Importance of Boundaries

The two most important things you can do to raise a child who is less vulnerable to grooming or abuse are to introduce the concept of boundaries and to open the avenues of communication. We'll start with boundaries.

Whether they are property lines, the limits of personal space, or national borders, people operate and thrive within boundaries. They help us focus, give us structure, and form the basis of civilized society. Boundaries protect us and empower us.

When my husband and I were pregnant with our son, we began to discuss discipline styles. I talked to him about the importance of schedules, rules, consistency, and accountability. I told him that children need clear, safe boundaries so they feel stable and protected. Only then can they learn to explore, push, grow, and expand. My husband thought I was nuts. He told me that he didn't want to run our home like a prison camp and that he believed that a child should have a free rein to grow. Clearly, he had no idea what I was trying to say.

I finally put my views into an example that he would understand: "On your first day of work at a new job, did the receptionist tell you, *Go sit anywhere and find something to do. Look for a boss. We have seventy-five departments. You will eventually find all of them, and I am sure there is a job for you in there somewhere. And yes, you will thrive in your career*"?

My husband sighed. "I get it," he replied. "We all need boundaries."

All of us are some kind of specialist, whether we are parents, engineers, doctors, administrative assistants, or plumbers. We choose our specialty and identify ourselves within that space. That's one boundary.

We don't let random people we don't know sit on our lap or stand two inches from our noses. We maintain our personal space. That's another boundary.

Our neighbors don't walk into our homes anytime they want at any hour of the day. Our home is private property, our safety zone that should be free from intrusion. That's another boundary.

We all have basic life boundaries, and they keep us secure and safe. And we can teach and learn boundaries right from birth.

Communication Is Key

Babies are great communicators. The first few months are tough as you learn baby's cries and signals. But as babies get older, they become a treasure chest of signs, signals, and sounds that tell you how they are feeling, who they like and don't like, and how they react to stimuli in their environment. No one will learn your baby's signs better than you will. Study those signs, encourage them, and shower love and attention on your baby anytime your baby tries to communicate with you, even if you have no idea what he or she is trying to say.

This is important for two reasons. First, communication is a gift that you will share with your baby for life. *Babies* who are loved and encouraged to communicate become *children* who know they are loved and who communicate with you. The more you support and encourage your growing baby to communicate with you—whether through coos, prattle, short sentences, or real discussions—the more likely it is that you will raise a child who tells you when he or she sees, hears about, or experiences something bad.

That brings us to the second point: If something does happen that affects your child's safety or health—whether it's abuse, trauma, or ill-ness—you will be the first to know and will be able to respond properly. Any pediatrician will tell you a story about the mother who brings in her seemingly healthy baby for an exam. On cursory examination, the baby looks fine. But the mother says, "See how my baby winces when she swallows? She has never done that before." Only a close and obser-vant caregiver who has studied the baby's signs and signals would be able to observe something like that and know to get the doctor's help.

Don't dismiss your baby when he or she speaks. Studies have shown that the interactions between infants and their primary caregivers affect how that baby will communicate with people for the rest of his or her life. Give your child every chance to learn that you want to listen.

There are babies who, due to illness, foster care, or other trauma, don't get the kind of communication opportunities I am talking about. But don't be discouraged if something stands in the way of commu-nicating with your baby. No matter where you are with your child or what your child's limitations may be, encourage and praise communi-cation, even when it's difficult and frustrating for you and your child.

When your child grows to trust you and share his or her feelings and thoughts with you openly, you'll be glad you did.

Consistency: Where Discipline Begins

At times, communicating with your baby or older child may prove to be a challenge. One of the theories of modern advertising tells us people need to hear something three times before they absorb the information in an advertisement or marketing campaign. Anyone who has dealt with children understands how often they fail to absorb and interpret information on the fourth or even fifth hearing. Not only do young children sometimes lack the skills to comprehend information as adults do, but they also live in a world full of stimulation, and their brains must filter out things that they don't seem to need. If the brain hears or feels something only once, it may not determine that it's important. By the third (or fourth or fifth) time, however, the brain may realize, "Hey, this is something that I should focus on."

Think about it this way: According to the "experts," we need to do an activity twenty-one days in a row to make it a habit. So creating the habits of communication and boundary setting is all about consistency and repetition. Consistency starts the development of self-control, body awareness, and the ability to thrive in a safe environment. Consistency is the key to discipline—not the textbook definition of punishment as a result of bad behavior. I am talking about the discipline of consistency and boundaries that you show your child. This type of discipline will empower your growing child. It will arm your child against anyone who tries to destroy those boundaries or to disrupt your lines of communication.

So how do the concepts of consistency and discipline apply to your baby?

Start with a Schedule

Your baby's development and security start with the schedule you set—your daily routine. For example, there's your feeding schedule: Your baby comes to expect to nosh at a specific time. Then there's the sleeping schedule: Your baby is put to bed at the same time so he or she develops consistent sleeping habits and learns to sleep for longer periods of time. A consistent napping schedule gives your child the benefit of interacting with his or her world without nodding off or being fussy or distracted. The most important thing about these schedules, however, is the security they provide.

You can tell your baby a million times, "I love you, and I will keep you safe and warm and fed and make sure you get lots of sleep," and chances are that your baby will understand little to none of it. But if you show your baby loving consistency, he or she knows instinctively that you will take care of specific needs at specific times. Baby's little body is free to adjust, grow, and develop without the pressures of wondering when and where the next meal or rest time comes. You've established boundaries, and baby will thrive within those boundaries. Consistency shows your child love and discipline. It builds trust between you and your infant, who relies on you for everything.

Show Loving Disapproval

By eight or nine months old, your baby is on her way to becoming a real person. She has ideas, wants things, and begins to push boundaries for the first time. Many parents say that babies are too young to understand right from wrong. But that is only partly true. The only way a child can learn right from wrong is from you.

It begins with discouraging simple things, like when baby pulls at your hair or pinches you with his tiny little fingers (my son's favorite thing to do at nine months). This is when you take baby's hand, kiss it, and say, "No, no, no," in a gentle way. Nearing the end of the first year, baby knows what "no" means. If baby keeps doing the bad behavior, then baby is gently put into the crib or set on a blanket on the floor.

What is happening? Baby is learning three important things: Bodies have boundaries, bad actions have consequences, and Mommy or Daddy disciplines with love.

How does this help against abuse? A child with strong body boundaries is less likely to be susceptible to grooming and sexualized behavior by adults. A child who is disciplined with love has behavioral boundaries within which to thrive. A baby who knows that certain behaviors are not acceptable, and that his parents will guide him or her appropriately, will grow into an empowered and confident toddler who is less likely to be abused.

Showing that you love your baby even though you disapprove of his or her actions is the beginning of discipline. Your baby wants your love and craves this structure, and you can provide it.

Memorize Your Baby's Body

Babies have little privacy and few boundaries when it comes to their bodies. As a primary caregiver, you touch, clean, and move almost every part of your baby's anatomy. When the weather is hot, you allow your baby to lie around naked. Family members and friends help, too, changing baby's diaper, giving baby a bath, and dressing and caring for the helpless infant.

But that doesn't mean your child is totally defenseless. Your baby has you.

Start with memorizing your baby's physique. Now is the time to completely examine and learn about your child's body. Write down important things like birthmarks or other characteristics that could help identify your child. Why? If you note a change and need to tell someone, you don't have to worry about forgetting anything in your distress and panic. You can also go to your pediatrician with a good chronicle of what you see, especially if the changes you have noted are due to another health condition that is worsening.

This kind of diligence will also help if you use any kind of care provider, especially one who is a mandated reporter. If your child's care provider notices anything, he or she can inform you, and you can work together as a team to protect the safety of your child.

Don't be embarrassed to calmly examine your child's genitalia and note any changes, problems, inflammation, or other condition. Discuss any and all concerns you have with your pediatrician. Don't worry if you think your question is dumb or silly. It isn't.

Keep your baby's genitalia clean and healthy. Note any discharge or other oddities. Manage diaper rash and heat rash as soon as you discover it. Encourage anyone who also changes your baby's diaper to do the same. Note and speak up if your child comes home from a care provider with excessive heat or diaper rash so you can ensure that your child and other children are properly cared for, no matter the caretaker.

Sure, you know what your child looks like. Sure, it can seem a little strange at first to be a "looky-loo." But it is unrealistic to keep your infant in your care twenty-four hours a day, every day of the week. You need to let your child's body do the talking until your child can speak for him- or herself.

No one wants to think about a baby being sexually abused. Some of the saddest cases I have worked with have been victims who were abused as babies. But if you know exactly what is going on with your child's body, you can intervene the second you notice something is amiss. Does this mean you should call the police anytime you see something different with your child's genitalia? No. It means you should go to your pediatrician, tell him or her what's going on, and take the appropriate next steps. I guarantee that the vast majority of the time, the changes will be perfectly natural or due to illness. But just in case, you want to be well-armed with information about how your baby's body may have changed.

Infants and Trauma

Science is only beginning to understand the effects of child stress and trauma on the brain. But they do know this: When you yell at your baby, yell around your baby, or expose your baby to chaos, you run the risk of creating real changes in your baby's little brain. I'm not talking about the normal yelling and screaming of older brothers and sisters—a reality that has been a part of babies' lives for time eternal. I'm talking about chaos and screaming associated with stressful situations. Studies have shown that trauma affects baby's brain development and can even activate genes that hinder a person's immunity and ability to handle stress.[11]

If there is chaos and trauma in your life that will affect your infant, get to the root of your problems and solve them. If you are in an abusive or a volatile relationship, fix it—or get out. In the meantime, during moments of chaos, take deep breaths and calm yourself down before picking up your baby. Do your best to never grab your baby or carry him when you are upset. It's impossible to remove all stress and chaos from a baby's life, but even small changes will make a difference.

Babies are not as resilient as we have been led to believe. They feel what they are exposed to and are affected by circumstances in their environment. What does this have to do with child sex abuse? If your baby is negatively affected by stress and chaos, he or she will grow into a more vulnerable child who may be more at risk of abuse.

Choosing a Day Care Provider

Few things are as stressful as choosing a care provider for your child, whether you work inside or outside of the home. Your baby is your treasure, your most prized possession—the last thing you want to do is hand him or her over to a total stranger. Unfortunately, we are not all multimillionaires who can stay at home and spend quality time with our children all day long. Even if you have the financial means to do

so, you may feel the need to work for your own personal growth and
well-being. Whatever the reason, choosing a care provider is one of the
most important decisions you can make. Don't take it lightly.

A day care center can be a place of joy for a child. It's no wonder:
Anyplace that is full of other children and mental stimulation will
naturally be one of your child's favorite places. As long as you do your
homework, of course.

How do you choose a provider with the goal of armoring your
child against abuse? Well, it's not much different from the process
of choosing a day care center that's safe, fun, and a positive learning
environment for you and your baby. You just have to know how to ask
the right questions and what to look for in a center. Here are some
suggestions:

- *Seek references.* This is a no-brainer. Your best source of
  information on day care providers is going to be other parents who have their children in day care.

- *Check with your local department of social services or a day care
  accrediting body.* If parents have lodged complaints or the
  center has been cited for bad or negligent practices, you will
  find information on it with these organizations.

- *Do research online.* You would be amazed at how often
  people neglect this simple task. Go to your favorite search
  engine and type in the name of the day care center followed
  by search terms like *abuse, sex abuse, lawsuit,* or *scandal.*

- *Take a tour of the facility.* Is the facility light, bright, and airy?
  Is it secure? What are the policies for pickup and drop-off?
  Are changing areas visible? Is there a schedule? Are there
  policies on who is allowed to be with the children? Does
  the facility do both criminal and civil employee background

checks? What are the sickness and injury policies? Who are
the facility's neighbors (in other words, is the building next
door to a halfway house, pot dispensary, or rehab facility)? If
the day care is operated by a church, do congregation members have access to the children (and if so, have they had
background checks)? If you can, meet the teachers, director,
assistants, and subs. If you have a good feeling about the
place, come back for a second visit.

- *What are the bathroom policies for older children?* Are children
supervised in the restroom? If children need help wiping,
are restrooms open so that a staff member and a child are
not alone behind closed doors?

- *Drop by the facility during a normal day.* Are you immediately
greeted at the door by an adult? Are you, a stranger, allowed
to wander among the children? Are the children in plain
view? Are they properly supervised? Are older children hiding from teachers or able to access a door leading outside? If
you can see the children, is there chaos, or are they engaged
in play? You can get a great feeling about the safety of a
facility with this kind of "drop in." If you see things that
set off alarms—like hiding children with access to exterior
doors—go elsewhere.

- *If you use an in-home day care, ask who else is allowed in the
home.* Ask if the provider can provide background checks for
other people in the home. If the caregiver has older children,
get specific information about the role those children play in
the care center. If they have any interaction with your child
or any other child, request that they be fingerprinted. If you
get pushback, go elsewhere.

Once you have chosen a day care facility you trust, hopefully you'll find out that you've chosen well. Still, you should continue to be alert to signs that things aren't right. Remember to do the following:

- *Trust your child's instincts.* Keep an eye out for complaints like these: "I just don't like it there." "Sometimes, I get scared." "I don't like (a particular teacher)." "It's dark and I'm alone." (Yes, that really happens.) Also, listen to your child if he or she shows fear about a teacher or another student.

- *Watch out for red flags.* Does your child cry and panic at drop-off time? At pickup, is your child smiling and happy? Is your child eating and sleeping well? Is your child hitting developmental milestones? Is your child lethargic, or does he or she have unexplainable marks? Are there changes to your child's genitalia? Have any other families left abruptly? Is your child losing weight? If you see any of these, go to your pediatrician immediately and report.

- *Don't worry about hurting someone's feelings.* If you don't feel comfortable sending your child to a particular day care center, then cut the ties with that facility right away. Choosing a school isn't about making other people feel good, following tradition, or embracing the prestige of a three-year waiting list. Your goals are safety, transparency, and openness among faculty and staff, and a loving and enriching environment for your baby.

Remember, your child's acceptance to Harvard has nothing to do with the day care center or preschool you choose. Any school that tells you differently has the wrong priorities. Your child's safety comes first, not the Ivy League.

Choosing a Nanny or Babysitter

Ninety-nine percent of the people who become child care providers do so because they truly love children. The person you hire may not be absolutely perfect, but if your child is safe, loved, cared for, given boundaries, enriched, and stimulated with play and learning, you have found yourself a winner.

Here are some tips:

- *If you use a service, make sure you get references on the actual service, as well as the nanny.* Talk to the references; don't just rely on a letter. Ask the tough questions. You'd be surprised how honest people will be.

- *Hire a nanny who has the necessary paperwork to live and work in the country where you reside.* It makes sense to avoid the entanglement of dealing with undocumented workers—plus, it's hard to do a background check on someone who has spent much of his or her life outside the country.

- *Make sure your sitter can communicate well in English.* If your child is injured, your nanny needs to be able to call you and emergency personnel and to communicate concerns or fears to you. If you already have a nanny who struggles with the language, help him or her get into classes to increase fluency. Encourage your nanny to learn—and he or she will share that encouragement with your baby.

- *Get criminal, civil, and driving record checks.* You can purchase these easily through numerous companies. Be sure to request civil court records. These can highlight all kinds of red flags that wouldn't be on a criminal check, like a messy divorce, crimes that are past the statute of limitations, and allegations of fraud.

- *Do an extensive interview.* Don't do it alone. Have your spouse, your partner, or a trusted friend help you with the interview.

- *Make it clear what your nanny's role is.* Is the caregiver also expected to do light housework? Are there places in the house that are off-limits? Do you mind if he or she cooks? The more upfront you are, the better the relationship you will have with your sitter, so that both of you can focus on what is important: your baby.

- *Stay at the house with the caregiver for the first week.* This is a great opportunity for you to get to know the caregiver, show your new employee around, and see how he or she interacts with the baby. But don't follow the caregiver around like a prison guard. Allow him or her to take the lead on care during that first week. This is also a great time for you to adjust to going back to work.

- *Install a nanny cam or a video baby monitor.* If you spend an entire week with your caregiver before leaving her alone with your baby, you will have a great perspective on your sitter's temperament, style, and interaction with your baby. But what happens when you are not around? While I am not a fan of spying, many people have had great success with nanny cams—mostly because they get to watch streaming video of their happy child all day long.

- *Follow your gut.* I cannot stress this enough. If something makes you feel on edge, address it immediately. Talk to your sitter. Be honest and be kind. Don't sit back and hope that things will clear up by themselves. Remember, your sitter is your partner. She is not just an employee; she is helping you raise your child.

After you have had your sitter for a while:

- *Talk to the neighbors who are at home when the caregiver is with your child.* I did this quite extensively when I had a nanny for my son. The neighbors loved my nanny and often commented on how she and my son were always smiling, laughing, and playing. They also mentioned how well behaved and sweet he was when he was with her.

- *Drop home unexpectedly.* Be upfront when you hire your sitter that there are times when you will "drop home" for a quick minute.

And all of the time:

- *Be fair and kind.* Pay well, and pay on time. A happy employee will be more likely to ensure your child is happy, too.

- *Monitor your baby.* A good sitter or nanny will be greeted by a happy child.

- *Empower your caregiver.* Show the sitter what consequences for bad behavior you use to lovingly discipline baby. Tell him or her it's okay to stick to strong boundaries and properly reward good behavior.

The number one defense your baby has is you. By being alert, knowing your baby, asking questions, and understanding what to look for in a caregiving situation, you can give your infant every chance to be safer from abuse. Your love, boundaries, and guidance are your best tools for raising a well-armored baby. You know the questions, you know the signs, and you have your gut. Use them all.

Chapter 10

First Steps: Teaching
Your Toddler to Be Safe

Oh no. This baby has legs. And he's not afraid to use them.

First your "baby" is walking; then he or she is running. Soon your toddler is in preschool—perhaps the first time he or she has been away from you for regular, prolonged periods.

Inside and outside of the home, this "perfect" child (in your eyes, at least) is now playing with and around older and younger children, sometimes just beyond your watchful eye. Your child has discovered your makeup drawers, the pots and pans, and crayons, and by now has left his or her mark (perhaps literally) on every part of your home.

Your child is tackling and achieving other huge milestones (or obstacles, depending on your child and his or her attitude about certain things): Grasping language and speaking in fuller sentences. Starting to use the potty—with success, at least some percent of the time. Perhaps your son or daughter has discovered the wonder of genitalia, and spends half of his or her waking hours with a hand down the pants. Running around the house naked after bath time has become an

Olympic event. You sigh. You laugh. And you love every minute you're spending with this amazing, growing creature.

The Magic of *No!*

Times have changed, and it's easier to inform and educate our children about things that may have embarrassed our parents and grandparents. We don't shame our children about their bodies. We don't tell them that wanting to know more about how their body works is nasty or naughty. Gone are the days (for the most part) when a parent or grandparent would keep a girl in the dark about her body until puberty, and then tell her only that menstruation is a cause for embarrassment or shame. If you have family members who do still feel shameful about their bodies or try to impart that shame to your child, be nice but firm in explaining the approach you have chosen for your child. One of the most important things we can do for our children is to remove shame from the discussion of our bodies. When we do that, we empower our children to speak up instead of shaming them into silence. Being a toddler and a preschooler is a magical time for a child. It's when a child gets a first taste of independence and learns that his or her actions have an immediate effect on other people. It's also the first time your child will stand up and say the *other* magic word—not *please*, but *no!*

And he or she will say *no!* a lot. Your child will say *no!* to food, to petting the dog, to taking a bath, to going to bed, to seeing Santa, to playing with other children. Most of the time, you'll manage to convince your child of the necessity of doing all these things—especially the eating, sleeping, and bathing parts. But sometimes you really should listen to your child's *no!* and recognize if there is a real reticence to what you are asking. If your child refuses to hug a friendly neighbor or be alone with a family member, consider and respect his or her wishes and fears. There may be something to them. Whether something has actually happened or it's just your child's "gut" talking, it's appropriate for you to respect your child's wishes.

Teaching your preschooler to be empowered is much easier than you think. It does not mean you will be raising a brat who is better suited for a television sitcom. Empowerment is about taking all the things that are beautiful about being a toddler and embracing them. It's about trusting your gut, using your eyes, and giving your child words to properly describe his or her world in a safe and consistent environment. Following are some lessons to help your child—and you—do just that.

Lesson #1: Understand Healthy Sexual Behaviors for This Age Group

Toddlers and preschoolers are biological creatures. They are learning that they have bodies and that those bodies have feelings, sensations, and physical responses. They will do things that feel good and give them physical pleasure, including touching their private areas. And they will do it at inappropriate times and in inappropriate places. This is a part of a child's healthy biological development. This does *not* mean that a child is sexual, wants to engage in sexual behavior, or has been exposed to or experienced abuse. Your job as a parent is to know what behaviors are natural, address the situation with your child, ensure that your child is never shamed for a healthy behavior, and make sure that certain behaviors are done in private.

If you see your toddler or preschooler touching him- or herself inside or outside of clothing, calmly and nicely tell your child, "We do not touch our penis or vagina when other people are around." Explain to your child that touching yourself gently is something private—that we don't do it at school, around our friends, in front of our parents, or in situations where anyone else can see.

It might be helpful to ask your toddler if he or she ever sees Mom or Dad touch themselves in public. When your child says no (probably while laughing, so feel free to laugh along), tell your child, "Of course. No one wants to see Mom walk around with her hands in her pants. And no one wants to see you do it, either." After a few times explaining, your child should "get it" and will know that although you are firmly establishing this boundary, you are loving, supportive, and willing to laugh.

Remember, a toddler who is touching him- or herself is not "horny" or overly sexualized. Your child is doing it because it feels good, just like a good back scratch or head rub. By simply encouraging your child not to engage in the behavior around other people, you do two things: 1) You allow your child to have a healthy and shame-free awareness of his or her body, and 2) you let your child know that this behavior should not be done around other people. As a result, if a predator tries to tell your toddler, "It's okay for you to do that around me," your child already knows that something is terribly wrong and will come to you and report.

There are many wonderful books and articles that explain the other healthy sexual behaviors for this age group and that point out warning signs or signals for parents. If your toddler or preschooler is engaging in a behavior that troubles you, talk to a therapist. He or she can help you determine whether there is a problem and go through the steps to address the issue, rule out abuse, and lovingly coach the child in changing the behavior.

Lesson #2: Use Correct Names for Body Parts

One of the easiest and best things you can do is teach your toddler the correct names of body parts. To some, this may seem a little odd. When I was a child, we didn't use words like *penis* or *vagina*—if we did, we usually got in trouble for it. Until somewhat recently, the true terms for human genitalia were used exclusively to talk about sex or in the medical realm. Growing up in past generations, we thought that they were "loaded" words, so we dumbed down our body parts and minimized their importance by using words like *wee-wee* or *hoo-hoo*. But we need to remember that our bodies should never be minimized and that these biological terms are correct and accurate.

This is important for a number of reasons. First, when you minimize something, it's not lost on your child. Kids are smart. They know that when you call something by a play name, then it's a plaything and not something important. But if you call something by a serious, "adult-sounding" name, your child is going to know that you mean business!

Children may not have highly honed reasoning or logic skills, but they instantly pick up on your language cues. Be vigilant. Our bodies are wonderful, but they are serious, and we shouldn't devalue them.

Second, using the correct names allows children to *own* their body parts, speak about them properly without shame, and draw appropriate boundaries with other kids and adults. Not only does this help protect against abuse, but it also helps on trips to the doctor, in playground accidents, and during "The Talk" ten years from now.

Remember, teaching the proper names of body parts does *not* mean that you should talk about sex with your preschool-aged child. Toddlers and preschoolers are way too young for any discussion of sex, even if they have walked in on you and your partner in the middle of a romantic interlude. With this age group, we are talking about body parts, not sexuality. Your son does not need to know what his penis will be used for later in life, and he will not ask. Your daughter does not need to know about the function of her vagina, but she does need to know its proper name and why she wipes herself to keep her vagina clean.

Once your child has the right names for body parts, he or she may start asking questions. Embrace these questions, and answer them as honestly and age-appropriately as you can. A girl with younger siblings may find out that a vagina is where a baby comes out of a mommy, but that's about the extent of what a child needs to know. And honestly, she will probably get distracted within seconds of you explaining it to her. But don't shut these questions down. Answer them as best you can and without shame.

Once you teach the proper names of parts and encourage questions, your child will probably come to you when he sees bumps, marks, or other things on his body that he didn't notice before. And if some of these marks require medical attention (things like infections, common viral issues like *Molluscum contagiosum*, rashes, painful skin tags, common penile abrasions, and bruises), you will be able to address these problems when they are small, and long before something like a vaginal infection (from incorrect wiping after using the toilet) becomes extremely painful and out of control.

Predators Love to Minimize Abuse

By calling body parts by play names, a predator can confuse a child into thinking that sexual abuse is a form of play and an expression of love. But when a predator tries to groom a child who knows the proper biological name for her vagina, for example, he won't be able to minimize the vagina's importance to the child and her body. There will be no question that her vagina and the area around it are *not* to be touched by anyone except in special situations, which only include Mom or Dad and the doctor (only when Mom or Dad are present).

Think about it this way: If you tell your child to call her vagina her *ha-ha*, it becomes easier for a predator to discover a way to make inappropriate touching seem acceptable. Here is a typical grooming tactic for a predator who targets toddlers and preschoolers: "I love tickling you, especially down there. I love how it makes you smile. What do you call that area?" Which child do you think is more likely to be abused?

Child #1: "It's my ha-ha."
Child #2: "It's my vagina. No one is allowed to touch me there."

The cops love parents who teach their kids the proper terms for their private parts. Which child do you think will be a better help to the police in prosecuting and jailing the molester?

Child #1: "He tickled my ha-ha. It made me laugh."
Child #2: "He tried to touch the area around my vagina. My mom says that no one is allowed to touch me there, so I told on him."

Parents Need to Get Over It

For parents of an older generation, it can be jarring to hear a little girl use the word *vagina* when talking about her body. To be honest, I am one of them. Growing up in a somewhat prudish Catholic home, we didn't use that word, even when we talked about sex. But I got over it. And so will you.

For a little girl, her vagina is another part of her body, like an arm or a leg. For a little boy, his penis is something that he can name and own. And by naming, owning, and drawing strong body boundaries around their genitalia, our children can better defend against a predator than the child who doesn't know what his penis or her vagina is, can't name it, has never talked about it with her parents, and doesn't understand that it is not okay for a predator to touch her there. For the child who is introduced to the proper terminology, it's not a loaded word. It has nothing to do with sex, purity, virginity, morality, or guilt.

So stop being embarrassed. As your child already knows, it's no big deal.

Lesson #3: Teach Your Child to Be Self-Sufficient in the Bathroom

Potty training can be one of the most frustrating chores of parenthood. And sometimes the lesson doesn't always stick. There are accidents, gross underpants in the laundry basket, and the occasional wet bed. And sometimes the gross underpants extend well into elementary school. Your child will not be perfect, and accidents will happen. But he or she should be as self-sufficient as possible, as quickly as possible, when it comes to using the toilet.

What do I mean by this? Encourage your child to wipe correctly as soon as he or she starts using the toilet. This lesson is even more important for girls, who need to be careful about hygiene and the health of their vagina and urinary tract. Fortunately, there is a wide variety of products on the market to help with this somewhat arduous task, including "kid-themed" bathroom products, extra-soft toilet paper, and wet wipes. You can even find recipes to make your own wipes if your child has delicate skin or if you prefer using more natural ingredients. Regardless, it's never been easier to be clean. (Thank goodness!)

As soon as your child starts using the toilet, begin teaching the proper way to wipe—especially with girls, who can develop infections if they don't wipe "front to back." Boys may be a little more reticent— on the whole, they tend to be less fussy about cleanliness than girls are. But if you encourage your child to wipe correctly and clean the private area well, you will give your child (and yourself) a whole new level of independence. And maybe your laundry won't be quite as gross.

What does this have to do with abuse? A common grooming technique for predators of young children is to gain the trust of a child enough to be able to wipe him or her after going to the bathroom. It's easy access that can quickly cross over into sexualized behavior. The sooner your child is independent, the less likely that a predator (who in these cases is usually a trusted family member) will have access to the child in the bathroom.

It's sad to think that a predator would do something like exploit a child in the bathroom. But your child does not have to be a target. Before your child is totally independent, monitor who helps your child in the bathroom. If an adult offering to help makes you feel "hinky," politely decline and do the job yourself. Also, be careful of "well-meaning" adults—for example, men without young children of their own, or a caring "grandparent" type who is no relation—who volunteer to take your toddler to the bathroom. Parents can barely stand the chore, so be cautious about enthusiastic volunteers.

Another reason predators target children who cannot care for themselves in the restroom is that a child who has irritated genitals because of poor wiping gives a predator an excuse to "examine" the child and offer to "help."

If you teach your child to be self-reliant—and to follow additional steps outlined later in this chapter—the bathroom can be a safe place for your child.

Lesson #4: Carefully Screen Preschools

Consider various preschools to ensure that you select one that meets every standard of safety for your child; you can use the same ideas and methods discussed in chapter 9 for choosing a day care provider. Many preschools require children to be potty trained before enrolling. The sooner you can help your child be self-sufficient in the bathroom, the better.

Here is a list of questions for you to consider when screening preschools. There are no hard-and-fast answers, but if you follow your gut and look at the school's safety policies, you can make a well-informed decision that will help keep your child safe.

- When you screen preschools, look for happy and engaged children. Are the adults smiling and happy with the children?

- Do you know other children who attend the school? Are their parents pleased with their child's education and happiness?

- Have any parents recently pulled their children from the school? Do you know why?

- Are doors open and windows clear of obstructions that would prevent someone seeing what is going on inside another room?

- Is there a constant and required "open door" policy? Are adults ever allowed to be alone with a child?

- How are medical needs on campus addressed? What happens if a child becomes ill at school?

- Are all adults who work with the children required to undergo civil and criminal background checks?

- Are the restrooms easily accessible for the children? What are the rules regarding using the toilet?

- On the playground, are children hiding, fighting, yelling, or out of control? Are playgrounds secure from strangers?

- Is there a sign-in and sign-out policy? Are parents allowed to observe the class?

- Have there been any civil lawsuits filed against the school?

- Have any teachers, aides, or volunteers been arrested for crimes on campus or involving children?

- What is the school policy regarding spouses and partners of teachers and aides? Are they allowed in the classrooms, and do they interact with children?

- Is there a written handbook of school rules and policies?

- If you have problems or issues with the school or an employee, will they be immediately addressed by teachers and administrators?

- If children are violent or show behavioral problems that endanger other children, how are these issues addressed?

- What is the school's abuse reporting policy and procedure? What has happened in the past in cases of seen or suspected abuse?

- How long have the teachers been at the school? Is there a heavy turnover?

- If the school is at a church, who hires the school director and church pastor? Do parent committees, a school board, or church members have the power to hire or fire?

- Does the school provide resources to parents about the community, parenting, safety, or other issues?

Lesson #5: Follow the "No Secrets" Rule

Kids, especially preschool-aged children, love the concept of secrets. It's their way of creating a child-centric world that is full of fantasy, play, and a child's sense of power. The problem is this: Secrets are a predator's pal. This is one of the most important things you can teach your toddler or preschooler.

There is a way to stop secrets and protect all of the children involved. It starts when your child is a toddler, with the "no secrets" rule. Simply tell your child that you live in a house full of love—and people who love each other do not keep secrets. I promise you, your three-year-old won't be confused or push back.

Your child will be aware and have her guard up when an adult tries to create or keep secrets with her. She will know that something is wrong and that adults never ask children to keep secrets. Hopefully, if this happens, the situation will be totally harmless. But if the situation is not harmless, your child is a hard target for a predator.

Your child will also have the tools and awareness to be able to come to you directly when an adult wants to keep secrets.

How a Predator Uses "Secrets"

Wrapping a child up in secrets and creating a special world that just the predator and the child share is the easiest way for a predator to gain a child's trust and ensure his or her silence. At first they're the child's innocent secrets—things like talking about scary nightmares, talking about Mommy and Daddy, or sharing information about another child. But then the adult takes control, and the secrets become bigger and more powerful. The predator will share his or her secrets with the child—things like how they are special friends, why their hugs feel so good, or something revealing about the predator (like bed wetting, self-touching, dreams, etc.) that the child is told not to share.

Now that the predator has earned the child's trust, he or she can be assured that the child will not talk about what the two of them do together, even if it turns into full-blown abuse. And because the adult has earned the child's trust, he or she can use threats to keep the child silent, telling the child something like, "Your mommy won't understand our special game, so don't tell her. She will get mad and punish us." Or the predator may go further and say, "Your daddy will get jealous and try to hurt me. If he does, he can go to jail. So don't tell him."

Keeping Another Child's Secrets

There will be some side effects once the "no secrets" rule goes into effect. If another child tries to create or keep secrets with your child, he or she will be told in a nice and loving way that people who care about each other don't keep secrets. For small children, this will start the momentum that can shut down secrets altogether in the peer group, and that's fine. Secrets are bad enough for younger kids. But if you don't address the problem of keeping secrets as your child grows older, secrets will only continue to cause problems for your child and threaten your child's (or another child's) safety.

Your growing child may encounter a peer who trusts and asks him or her to keep secrets about sexual abuse, other crimes, domestic violence, or drug abuse. And if your child agrees to keep the secret, he or she unwittingly becomes a part of the problem. The secret teller will feel much better by confiding in your child—lightening his or her load and creating an ally who understands the situation and agrees to remain quiet. But the ten-ton weight has been moved from the shoulders of your child's friend . . . and placed directly on your own kid's shoulders.

Children and teens don't create these webs of secrets on purpose or with any kind of maliciousness. They do it because they are young, they are scared, and they don't know any better. But you *do* know better and can stop this cycle before it starts.

A Secret Is Not a Surprise

Tell your toddler or preschooler that secrets are different from surprises. A surprise is something that will be revealed to everyone at just the right time—things like birthday and Christmas presents and surprise parties. Surprises are fun and make people smile. Surprises always have a big reveal, and everyone is happy to learn about them.

Revealing surprises at the right time doesn't hurt feelings, scare people, or make people mad.

Secrets, on the other hand, do not make people happy. They keep people far away. Sometimes secrets are about things that can hurt us. They can scare people. That's why we always need to tell and we never keep secrets. We don't keep secrets, so people won't get hurt and we can solve problems and help everyone.

You can teach your child the difference between secrets and surprises. You won't need to do much more explaining. If your preschooler repeatedly asks, "Why?" just tell him or her that people who love each other do not keep secrets. They share with each other. You can also tell your child that adults who want to keep secrets with a child may want to hurt the child, and that is why it is always so important to tell Mommy or Daddy anytime an adult or anyone else wants your child to keep a secret.

Child sexual abuse is a crime of shame and secrecy. If you take away the power of the secret, suddenly the predator has one less tool of manipulation. So no secrets, ever.

Lesson #6: Establish Boundaries for Privacy

Toddlers love to look and touch. They love to run around naked, see how their body works, feel warm and cool air on their skin, and be free within their bodies. Within the home, they should be able to relish that freedom and the ability to discover their bodies without shame. The whole world, however, is not as safe as the home.

Your job as a parent is to help your child draw proper and safe boundaries, understand the privacy and sanctity of his or her body, and communicate right and wrong behaviors. When you teach your child boundaries, he or she can thrive safely and still retain the innocence and joy he or she deserves.

Embrace the Bath: Lessons on Touching and Looking

Teaching privacy boundaries is quite easy, and the bathtub is your friend. Because younger children need to be supervised in the tub, they love to play, talk to you, and listen to your stories while they bathe. You already know this—a ten-minute bath becomes hours long as you talk about your child's day, sing songs about letters and numbers, make animal noises, and laugh about silly stuff. What better time to introduce lessons about body safety?

A good place to begin is with a discussion of touching. In the course of a normal bath conversation, it's easy to tell your child, "You know that no one is allowed to touch you if you do not want them to, right?" Wait for your child's answer. He or she will probably say yes, and you can end the lesson for the day.

Another time, you can insert specifics about the areas of the body that no one should ever touch—the child's genitals, breasts, etc. But take it one sentence and one bath at a time. Don't overwhelm your child. Make these lessons small and transparent, inserted between discussions of "What does the cow say?" and "Who did you play with today?"

As you progress over the course of a few weeks or months, tell your child, "We never touch anyone else's genitals inside or outside of their clothes." Following this statement with, "Blech! That's icky!" will also get the point across that not only is it "not nice" to touch other people's genitals, but it's as gross as picking noses or eating worms. Make sure your child understands that this rule also applies to kicking or punching. Tell your child that if he or she sees anyone punch or kick anyone else in the genitals, he or she must tell you or a teacher immediately.

Make the lesson a slow process that is natural and casual. Your child will not feel weird, and you can be confident the lesson is sinking in.

The issue of "looking" is much more dynamic. Anyone in a family situation knows that nudity happens, especially when there are very young children in the house or a new baby is born. But it is okay to tell your child that no one outside the family should see him or her naked. Usually, your child will naturally become more aware of his or her body by age three or four. Around that time, your child may embrace modesty outside of the home and will not want people to see his or her naked body—for example, at the pool without a bathing suit or while changing clothes. This is a good behavior that you should support as much as possible. Make sure your child understands that his or her body is beautiful and private, and encourage your child to embrace that body privacy.

This is also a good time to encourage your child to respect the privacy of other children, especially non-siblings, by not looking or staring at them when they are not clothed.

Just like those on touching, these lessons can be short, happy, and reinforced often and in situations that are appropriate. Never use shame or tell a child that his or her body is a cause for embarrassment. Instead, explain that privacy is beautiful, and that adults outside of the home should never see her naked. Feel free to insert your exceptions; maybe Grandma helps with bath time or a trusted adult caregiver helps your child change clothes. But when it comes to people outside the immediate family and trusted caregivers, the hard and fast rules should apply: no looking, no touching. The daily and much-loved post-bath "naked dance" should be embraced, just not when there are unfamiliar adults in the home.

Around the age of six, your child will begin to notice that your adult body is very different from his young body. This is usually a good time for parents to enforce their own privacy when it comes to nudity. Like many other areas of parenting, there are no hard-and-fast rules. In fact, when there are other young children in the house, this can be close to impossible. So be as flexible as you need to be. And if your family embraces nudity in the home, that is fine. Just be sure that your child enforces his or her privacy when *not* in the home.

Set the privacy boundaries early on, and they will last throughout childhood. Your toddler or preschooler is smart and will listen. The only mistake you can make is not talking about privacy at all.

Create Safe and Happy Pictures

The age of the Internet has changed the dynamic when it comes to taking pictures of children. When I was a child, it was standard procedure to take photos of naked kids in the bathtub. Nowadays, things are different.

It is still fine to take pictures of small children in the tub, but be sure that their genitals are not in the photos (especially if these photos are going to be shared, texted, emailed, or posted on the Internet). It's simple and easy to do, and you can still create all of the fun memories of bath time. In this age of easily copied digital photos, however, remember that you are the gatekeeper of your child's privacy and digital footprint. The more you can do to create safe and happy photos, the safer your child's online digital life will be.

But the picture lesson goes far beyond family time.

Pornography is *not* your picture of a child in the bathtub, but is far more ugly and graphic. You and your child do not need to discuss child pornography or why it is a crime. In fact, this discussion will not be age-appropriate for many years—not until your child starts to use the Internet and runs a serious risk of stumbling across it. But you can lay good protective and empowering building blocks when your child is a toddler and preschooler.

Tell your child that no one is to take pictures when he or she has no clothes on—and if it happens, your child should always come and tell you. That's all you have to say.

If you approach this rule the same way as you approach the rules of crossing the street or sharing toys, your child will not be scared or threatened. Your child doesn't have to learn about the horrors of child pornography. They just need to know that their body is beautiful and private and that no one ever should take pictures of it when the child has no clothes on.

Lesson #7: Begin the Discussion about Trusted Adults

There are adults in your child's life who are considered "trusted adults": non-immediate family members who are strong, loved, trusted, and empowered to protect the well-being of your child. This can be a childhood friend, a cousin, or another adult to whom you turn in times of crisis. This is the childhood friend who was there for your child's birth, the sorority sister you trust implicitly, your closest cousin, or a friend who is a parent and who shares your views on child safety. You know who these people are in your life.

About the time your child hits preschool, it's good for your child to know that if you are not there, he or she can go to this trusted adult. Tell your child that if he or she is hurt or scared and the trusted adult is around, it is safe to talk about what has happened.

Other trusted adults in your child's life can be teachers, police officers, day camp counselors, pastors, and so forth. Now, I am sure you have discovered the problem here: These "trusted adults" are also the kinds of people who might gain a child's trust in order to abuse. Unfortunately, that is true. But this is where your role as an informed and empowered adult comes to bear. Because you know and understand the signs of grooming, and because you are learning to trust your gut when it comes to predators, you are going to be able to better tell and understand who should be the trusted adults in your child's life. Always do your research. Learn about the adults who spend time with your child, and look closely at the institutions (camps, schools, etc.) where your child spends his or her time.

Lesson #8: Don't Force Hugging and Kissing

As a child, I hated hugging old men. It wasn't because I thought they were creepy or had a bad experience with an older man when I was a young child. My reason was pretty simplistic: I hated the way I smelled afterward. Usually, it was a mixture of Old Spice, cigarette smoke, and mothballs. And here is what made it worse: I was always forced to hug these men anyway.

My parents never meant any harm. They just didn't want to hurt anyone's feelings and thought that these hugs were totally harmless. They just wanted me to be a "nice little girl." But the lesson I learned was far more insidious. In my little mind, I learned that when an adult wanted to touch me in a way I didn't like, I had to submit. If I didn't, I would hurt their feelings and disappoint my parents. What they did (as tens of millions of parents across the country have done) was communicate to me that I didn't have the right to say no if an adult wanted to touch me in a way I didn't like. It was a lesson that would haunt me later in life.

Do not force your child to hug or kiss anyone. Hugging and kissing adults are not signs of respect. They are not signs of love when the child is forced or unwilling. And when you tell your child that adults don't have to respect his or her body boundaries, you are doing the predators' work for them. Let your child politely say no. Teach him or her that saying no to kissing or hugging is okay. If children learn that their space and body are respected, they are far more likely to understand and appreciate proper boundaries with all adults.

What do you do to replace the unwanted hug? Teach the handshake. Enforce the rule of eye contact and the smile. Don't want to deal with germs? Teach your child to say, "Very nice to see (or meet) you," and then tell the adult that your child is a petri dish of germs from school and that you don't want to share any of the local viruses. The adult will gush over your polite child and thank you for your consideration, and everyone will win. Even a "fist bump" with eye contact and a smile is a great and respectful way for a young child to greet an adult, especially if your kid has the sniffles or it's flu season.

Lesson #9: Embrace the Tattletale

I have been blogging steadily since 2010. While my blog, *The Worthy Adversary*, started as a commentary on the sexual abuse crisis in the Catholic Church and other institutions, my posts evolved over time to cover more parenting and abuse-prevention issues. Far and away my most popular post to date is about tattletales.

I love tattletales. I embrace them and foster their behavior. Am I nuts? Far from it. If there was one thing you could do *right now* that would empower our nation's kids, help prevent sexual abuse, hinder bullies, put criminals behind bars, and foster corporate and organizational transparency, you would do it, right? Well, you know how to do that? We have to stop punishing our tattletales.

When toddlers or preschoolers come to you and say, "He called me a name," "She won't share," "He's crying," "They were hitting," they need your help to solve a problem. It is our job as parents to get to the root of the problem. We can use this teachable moment to show our children how to solve problems so the kids can get back to the business of playing.

Why do kids tattle? Most of the time it's about the small stuff—the stuff that is stopping the fun. Kids just want to play, and they don't want naughty behavior to ruin it. Kids want their peers to know that everyone needs to be nice, behave in a positive manner, and cooperate. The tattlers are setting the bar for their peers. They are doing something else as well: They are being transparent about it.

But when we punish tattletales, we are teaching our children to turn a blind eye to wrongdoing. *We are teaching them that reporting wrongdoing is just as bad as committing the crime.* And when we do that, we foster cover-up and enable predatory behavior and all other kinds of wrongdoing. We need to start thinking about tattling in a different way: It's the closest thing that children have to "mandatory reporting."

I have asked numerous adults why they punish tattletales. I make sure to stress that in my hypothetical situation, the tattletale is telling the truth and wants to report behavior that is wrong. Their typical response: "Because tattling is wrong. No one likes a tattletale." Here's what the child hears: *If you report wrongdoing, no one will like you.* Is that a lesson we want our kids to take into adulthood?

Remember, childhood sexual abuse, bullying, and other crimes that plague our children thrive in secrecy. These crimes thrive in a world where kids are scared to talk to an adult. They thrive in a world where "tattletales" are punished. If we tell our kids not to tattle on their peers, will they tell someone later when they learn that a friend is being sexually abused? Or if they see a peer beating up another child? Or if they know a child who is responsible for cyberbullying a classmate?

What happens when our children grow into adulthood and see criminal behavior at work? Or when, as adults, they suspect sexual abuse? Is that tattling too? How do they know the difference?

If you want your toddler or preschooler to be comfortable telling you about things, you can't punish the child for reporting the bad things he or she sees and hears. In fact, if you want to foster communication with your growing child, you need to embrace these tattletale moments. Use them to help your child learn to solve problems, especially if the child is tattling in order to seek attention. Continually reassure your child that being transparent and truthful is an admirable quality. After all, honesty and refusal to turn a blind eye to wrongdoing are qualities that will keep your child safer from grooming, predators, and bullying, and will benefit him or her throughout life.

Lesson #10: Keep an Eye on the Peer Group

Your toddler or preschooler is starting to have friends and develop a peer group, whether at school, at day care, at church, in the neighborhood, or through other organizations. Your child will probably prefer the company of some children over others, and he or she will not be alone. The truth is, in these groups, there will be kids whom you do not like.

Don't feel guilty for disliking the behavior of other children. It's virtually impossible to change another person's parenting style and even harder to control an out-of-control preschooler, especially when that preschooler does not belong to you. If you do not want a certain child to be around yours, politely say no to playdates or compassionately address the other child's behavior with teachers or caregivers.

You will see red-flag behavior in other children. This may be aggression—whether general or specific (e.g., hitting or kicking the genitalia)—inappropriate language, acting out, and so forth. If you see any of these behaviors, be sure to tell the parents of the child who is engaging in them. Be gentle—the parent may be unaware or may become defensive. The parent may get offended or may ask for help. Be prepared for either outcome.

If the matter is not resolved, pull your child out of the situation, whether it's switching to another play group or avoiding the playground at a certain time. This may seem like a hassle—for example, when it means changing to another day care provider. But if you continue to allow your child to be in situations where he or she may get hurt, your child is going to think that it is better to not cause problems and is going to feel powerless when other children try to hurt him or her.

Sometimes being around naughty, aggressive, or troublesome children is unavoidable. Be honest with your child and talk to him or her about the problem. Ask whether your child knows why the other child acts the way he or she does. Problem-solve with your child—see if you can find a solution together. But whatever you do, tell your child that his or her safety and happiness are always your first priority.

Preschool peer groups also may bring you into contact with parents you may not like. You may see behaviors with the adults that make you uncomfortable or make you feel "hinky." Again, it's time to trust your gut. If you don't like a child's parents or their actions, politely decline invitations and never allow your child to be alone with those parents and their child. If you are kind and apologetic about it, you won't ruffle any feathers. But stand firm. Remember, you are your child's first (and sometimes only) line of defense. Don't put him or her at risk simply because you fear hurting someone's feelings.

* * *

The preschool years are a magical time. You will never laugh so much, smile so often, and want to bang your head against the wall—all within a two-hour period—as you will with your toddler. Even though you may feel like you have no control over this small bundle of energy, it takes only a few small, simple changes to ensure his or her safety.

Chapter 11

A Big, New World:
Elementary School Days

It's happened. Your child has become a "person."

This creature, who just yesterday was toddling around your house saying *no!* to everything and whose boo-boos were cured with a kiss, is now a thinking, feeling, semilogical stakeholder in your household. This child has real and valid opinions. While you remain the parent and authority, you now find that your kid has pretty decent input on bigger issues than just what color of socks to wear.

And like your toddler, this growing child earns new freedoms every day. Sometime between ages five and ten, he or she may start walking to school, playing in the front yard while you are inside, or riding a bike to soccer practice. At some point during this stage, your child may also be ready to go on sleepovers, camping trips, and overnight school field trips. Your child is starting to enjoy these new freedoms.

But your child is probably sharing less and less of his or her day with you. The chatty preschooler who used to tell you about coloring and butterflies and dinosaurs may now answer your questions with only "Yeah" and "Nope." Your child needs you more than ever but doesn't quite know how to show you. Even while trying to learn to be a "big boy" or "big girl," your child really wants you to hold his or her hand as much as possible . . . as long as no one else can see.

Helping and armoring your elementary school–aged child is easier than it looks. With small and subtle changes in the way you talk to your child and acknowledge his or her input—while remaining a parent and providing boundaries that allow him or her to thrive—you can still protect and empower your five- to ten-year-old. You can help your school-aged child navigate his or her world and stay safer from abuse.

The goal of this chapter is to help you make your child a "hard target" for predators. Creating a hard target is much more than teaching him or her about predators or warning about "stranger danger." It's about creating a home where you—as the parent or caregiver—are there to provide for your child's emotional needs. It's about creating a communication strategy so your child knows that he or she can trust you and that you will take any concerns, fears, and input seriously.

An Era of Responsibilities

This is a magical age. Now your child has responsibilities at home, complete with rewards and consequences. While teaching your child to do chores will make your job harder at first, with careful cultivation, your child can become a big help around the house. In a short time he or she will be doing chores and duties that are age-appropriate and will help prepare him to be able to cook, clean, and do laundry after moving out of the house someday. This is where you help your child start down the path toward becoming a functioning adult.

A six-year-old child is perfectly capable of putting away his or her own laundry (maybe with a little guidance) and bringing in the empty garbage cans (if they are on wheels or if this is not beyond the child's physical abilities). A child this age can be responsible for his or her own homework and setting and clearing the table for a meal. This is simple stuff that can help lighten a parent's load. In return, it's perfectly reasonable for the child to receive a small allowance or special "perks" (an extra story at bedtime, additional video game time, etc.) as a reward for doing these chores.

The benefits of this are myriad. First, these kinds of chores make your child a partner in household tasks. A child who appreciates the work involved in how a household runs will have more respect for his or her parents because the child sees how hard they work. Being an adult who has a job, pays the bills, and maintains the household is hard enough. But juggling that with parenthood is no job for sissies. Making your child pull his or her own weight in age- and skill-appropriate ways will help your child learn respect, compassion, and the value of every member of the household. No one wants to raise a child who expects to have everything handed to him or her on a silver platter. Chores are a great way to start.

But what does this have to do with creating a "hard target?" Everything.

Close your eyes for a moment and think about what you are most proud of—emotionally and physically. Whether it's your family, your career, or a big accomplishment, I am going to bet it was something that you worked hard to earn, right? No one says they are "proud" they won the lottery or proud they are a trust-fund baby. But people *do* say they are proud of their family, the home they work hard to own or rent, their career achievements, their college degrees, their other awards and milestones, and their healthy relationships. When you work hard to earn something, you carry that pride with you. You stand taller, you have confidence, and you are less susceptible to sadness or manipulation. This phenomenon is no different for your child.

A child who helps the family and is rewarded for doing so builds confidence. The child builds self-esteem from knowing that his or her hard work matters to the household. The child also learns that there are benefits and perks to hard work, beyond the pride of achievement. This self-esteem and confidence will bleed over into other areas of a child's life. Children who know they are important and their input and work are valued are less likely to fall for the flattery, manipulation, or gifts that a predator may try to shower on them. Children who earn money at home will find it odd when an adult gives them money or gifts they did not earn, and these children will be less likely to accept those kinds of gifts. Children who receive proper accolades for real contributions and hard work at home and school are more likely to look askance at an adult who showers them with flattery for things like "maturity" or good looks.

Children also build tremendous self-esteem through sports, martial arts, hobbies, teamwork, and learning. Such activities bring their own challenges, responsibilities, and rewards. Anytime a child is encouraged to stretch him- or herself and achieve, that child builds healthy self-esteem. The physical self-confidence your child gains through martial arts and other classes is also a powerful tool against bullying and manipulation. Chores, sports, and hobbies aren't a foolproof answer, but they are a building block—a layer of the armor that can protect your child from predators and their grooming behaviors. And the earlier you start setting up responsibilities for your child, the more protected your child will be.

A Word about Grace

Now that your child is in elementary school, you may see situations that frustrate you, confuse you, make your blood boil, or make you wonder if you are sane. Your key to getting through these moments—especially with teachers, school administrators, or other parents—will be handling the situation with grace and tact.

If something happens at your child's school or playground that angers you, stay strong and try not to react emotionally. Yelling and finger-pointing will only push others to go on the defensive and refuse to help. Anger and blame will also confuse and alienate your child, who will avoid coming to you with problems if he or she fears that you are going to overreact. Your child may also fear the blowback of being punished by others for your actions and reactions. So take a deep breath, swallow hard, slap on a smile, and calmly but firmly enforce change—over time, if necessary.

School—and All That Comes With It

Peer groups, the Internet, sex education, puberty, sleepovers . . . Your elementary school–aged child is surrounded by opportunities for learning, good and bad. These opportunities aren't limited to children who attend public school; even homeschooled children will be exposed to the big, wide, sometimes age-inappropriate world through their peers, technology, and television. The best thing parents can do is address each of these issues head-on.

Your five- to ten-year-old is coming into contact with more people than ever now. You cannot choose the children who attend school or other group activities with your child. You can't choose how those children are raised, what their parents think is appropriate, the language those children use at home, or how those children interact with your child on the school grounds. But you can be a proactive advocate for your child by teaching good decision-making skills and building partnerships with your child's teachers, schools, and other influences.

Here are some things you can do to help understand and deal with what is happening at school.

School Lesson #1: Ask Your Child Open-Ended Questions

Instead of "How was your day?" (*Fine*) or "Did you have a good day?" (*Yeah*)—ask specific, open-ended questions: "What did you play at recess?" "Who played with you?" "It was really hot today. What did you do after lunch to cool down?" Listen to your child's cues. With the right questions, asked in nonthreatening ways, you can learn all about the social intricacies of the second grade, why a certain kid is always in trouble, or how your child deals with conflict on the playground. Even a kid who normally clams up and doesn't volunteer information will be happy to tell you all about the rules of the latest playground game—and then will go on to tell you about every kid who plays it. Why? Because you are interested in what your child is interested in.

School Lesson #2: Seize the Conversational Moments

Once you pry open your normally clammed-up kid by asking open-ended questions, now is *not* the time to check your smartphone, disengage, or suddenly become too busy to hear your child out. Remember, predators know what children like to talk about. They also know how to ask the right questions and make time to listen to a child's answers. The only way to prevent a predator from gaining that foothold is to seize those moments yourself when your child opens up to you.

The best conversations—the ones where your child will talk about potentially embarrassing, troubling, or scary things—will happen when your child is at his or her most relaxed and feels completely safe. For many kids, this is at bedtime, when a child is tucked in, the lights are off, and Mom or Dad is there to say good night. Yes, sometimes this is also a stall tactic, but if your child wants to talk about a school bully for five minutes, allow him or her to be awake and engaged with you for a few minutes after "lights out." Seven- or eight-year-olds typically aren't long conversationalists. They just want to tell you something that bothered them or is important to them. They want you to listen and help. Don't dismiss it when they reach out to you.

School Lesson #3: Put on Your "Observing Glasses"

You can learn a lot at school pickups and drop-offs. Whether you are fortunate enough to share this time every day or you only get to do so once in a while, arrive early if you can. This is a wonderful opportunity to observe your child in his or her "natural habitat."

You don't need to hold your child's hand and walk him or her to class—by the second grade, most children will have none of that anyway! All you need to do is observe what your child does and where he or she goes. With whom does your child talk, laugh, and play? How does he or she look while doing it? Is your child smiling? Do other children and parents seem happy? Are playground or schoolyard supervisors watching what's going on, and are they happily engaged? Are kids hiding from one another or from adults? Do you see pushing, exclusion, or other red-flag behaviors?

Note everything you see. If you see anything dangerous, tell the school immediately. If you see anything that intrigues or mildly concerns you, ask your child about it. Questions can be as simple as, "I noticed that So-and-so looked kind of sad today, and none of the other girls were talking to her. What happened?" You'll find out whether the child in question just has a cold or whether the other girls are mean to her.

While you can't solve all the problems in the schoolyard, you can help your child make good decisions about how to deal with issues he or she faces at school. You can answer, "That's sad that the other girls aren't talking to So-and-so. That happened to me once in the second grade. I bet she just wants someone to say hi to her and walk with her to class." Your child will know that you care and are engaged, and may be more likely to come to you if he or she is having issues on the schoolyard.

Observe the behavior of other parents, too. By watching, you might learn some great tactics that other parents use in challenging situations. Of course, you'll see other parenting approaches that you do not agree with, as well. You cannot teach other people how to parent, but it could be helpful to note parents whose style may not be in sync with yours.

School Lesson #4: Partner with Your Child's Teacher

Make it clear from day one that you want to create a partnership with your child's teacher. Being a teacher is often a thankless, more-than-full-time job. Many elementary school teachers have to buy their own classroom supplies and get little support from administration. Plus, they have to deal with twenty or thirty sets of overworked, anxious, and needy parents daily. Let's not forget how tough it is to manage one seven-year-old, let alone a herd of them. Your child's teacher could probably use a partner.

You will not always agree with how your child's teacher handles things. So how do you deal with this? Treat your child's teacher like the professional colleague he or she is. Your child's teacher is not your employee, but your partner. Think about it: You don't agree with everyone at your workplace—and sometimes you learn that your assumptions and conclusions are wrong. But you can only learn that through discussion and compromise. So if you have learning-related, classroom, or playground issues, open up a discussion with the teacher. Create opportunities for problem-solving, and work together for change. Once you do that, the teacher will feel more comfortable communicating all kinds of things that can help make sure your child is safe, happy, confident, and learning.

Try to volunteer in your child's class, even if you have to take time off work to do it. Chances are that your child will act differently with you in the classroom, but volunteering in the classroom will give you an indication of the dynamics among the children who attend school with your child. It also shows both your child and your teacher that you care and are engaged.

School Lesson #5: Don't Hesitate to Raise the Red Flag

You are becoming a well-armored parent, so you are going to start seeing things that other parents may dismiss as "natural." If you see grooming behaviors—manipulation, flattery, a teacher or other school employee spending inappropriate time with a student or students—report the behavior right away to a school administrator. If your concerns are not addressed, or if the behavior continues or escalates, contact Childhelp at 1-800-4-A-CHILD. Likewise, if you see dangerous behaviors like harassment, bullying, an unsafe classroom, or criminal behavior, report to law enforcement *and* administrators right away. Don't back down even if someone else considers it "overreacting;" you know what you've seen, and now you know where it can lead.

School Lesson #6: Remember That the Power of Your Child's Education Is in Your Hands

If your child is bullied or is the victim of any kind of abuse in school—or if your child witnesses any abuse—the problem needs to be dealt with immediately and completely. I have dealt with dozens of victims whose parents knew of or reported abuse and trusted that school or church officials would take care of the problem. But guess what—they didn't. I cannot stress this point enough: *No one is going to advocate for your child like you are.* Your child's future is in your hands—not the school's or other bureaucracy's. If there is a problem, address it and follow up on it. If it involves criminal activity, call the police. If the problem is not fixed, find a better school for your child. Don't sacrifice your child's safety and happiness because of your loyalty to a learning system or an institution.

School Lesson #7: Don't Be a "Helicopter Parent"

While observing, reporting on, and being engaged with your child's school is essential, try not to be a "helicopter parent" who hovers over your child every second of every day. You can be observant and engaged without being intrusive or domineering. You can drop your child off at school and carefully observe the atmosphere without carrying the backpack, walking your child into the classroom, helping your child put books away, and telling your child the order in which to eat the contents of her lunch. Being a powerful and protective parent means offering your child appropriate freedoms and responsibilities, while still being vigilant. If you baby your child instead of allowing the child to take care of his or her own needs, your child will not learn the skills or have the confidence necessary to repel a predator.

School Lesson #8: Listen to the Gossip Mills

Gossip is not always a bad or vindictive thing. When the rumor mill spins tales about children who may be hurt or threatened, you can help by acting on those tales. In fact, it's your duty and obligation to address the situation immediately. In my own case, parents had heard rumors that a high school teacher was sexually abusing numerous girls, but instead of trying to learn more, discovering that the rumors were indeed true, and reporting to the police, they did nothing. If rumors are about something that might affect children, get down to the truth and report.

Listening to the rumors doesn't mean you have to believe everything you hear. But there is almost always a small grain of truth to a rumor, and an engaged parent will make sure that the "grain" is not something that puts any child in danger.

School Lesson #9: Demand Transparency

As a parent, you have a right to ask for the truth about decisions that school administrators make. You also have a right to honest and complete information about any aspect of a school decision that affects your child.

Here is an example: A school fires a hot lunch provider because one of the children was poisoned by salmonella due to negligence. Instead of being honest and telling parents why the provider was fired, the school keeps the issue under wraps. But what if other children were poisoned and their parents didn't know it was due to the hot lunch provider? What if that lunch provider goes on to another school and poisons children there? An elementary school that is not transparent when it fires a food service provider might not be transparent about other things that affect student safety.

Transparency is key. The best way to ensure that you have all the information you need is to *get involved*: Join PTA/PTL/PTO organizations. Attend school board meetings. Read school newsletters. Talk to your child's principal. And all the time, ask the tough questions. If you are stonewalled, demand answers and do not give up. Secrecy has no place in a school.

School Lesson #10: If the School Has Covered Up a Past Scandal, Consider Sending Your Child Elsewhere

Yes, sex abuse is everywhere—that is an unfortunate truth. But when schools cover up sexual abuse, and especially when administrators are not held accountable or removed for their transgressions, there is a systematic problem and all children there are at risk. This is especially a problem in schools with a huge alumni base and large tuition, or in areas where parents put too much trust in local districts. Many administrations have gotten away with a public apology and a promise to make changes. Regrettably, in my years of experience, when administrators who cover up abuse are allowed to remain in their positions, not much changes.

If your child's school had any kind of sex abuse cover-up scandal in the past, consider sending your child elsewhere for his or her education. There are plenty of good schools out there where administrators and educators have not covered up abuse. One of those schools will make a better educational home for your child.

A Note on Sex Education

Sex education in schools is a controversial topic. I will not open a can of worms by getting into the pros and cons here, because that discussion is not directly related to this book. But I will say this: Girls and boys develop at different ages and different speeds. While you may think your ten-year-old boy is way too immature for sex education, he may attend classes with girls who are already menstruating. While your older elementary school–aged child may not be ready for the "big talk," it may be time for him or her to learn about puberty and the changes that everyone's bodies will soon be going through.

Peer Groups—and All That Comes With Them

Puberty for your child may begin in elementary school. Unfortunately, elementary school is also where drama begins. Peer groups develop more specific characteristics and become more important, bringing with them a lot of love and pain. For girls especially, no matter how hard you try to avoid it, cliques happen. Little girls will shut out certain peers, develop petty jealousies, and cause heartache. Meanwhile, boys will get into fights, get their feelings hurt, and be teased for crying. Other parenting books can help you address these issues in greater depth, but for the sake of this book, we'll simply consider how you can approach your child's peer group with an eye to reducing his or her vulnerability to sexual abuse.

Peer Group Lesson #1: Keep a Close Eye on Your Child's Peer Group

You will not be able to control your child's play group at school. As you did for your toddler and preschooler, however, you can be observant and monitor who he or she plays with at home, whether yours or theirs.

There will be children that you do not want playing with your child. It is perfectly reasonable to find compassionate ways to make sure your child does not spend time with children you consider troublemakers or dangerous. It is also perfectly fine to be honest and firm with children—yours and their friends—in your own home.

Peer Group Lesson #2: Prepare for Sleepovers and Extended Time in Other Homes

Sleepovers and long playdates are a precious and important rite of passage for this age group. In these situations, children learn important socialization skills, are exposed to new foods and cultures, and see their imaginations soar. For parents, however, sleepovers are also scary and exhausting. While your child may be too young for sleepovers at age five, he or she may be a regular by age ten, when kids begin to form strong bonds of friendship.

How to Prepare Yourself for Your Child's Sleepover

Before your child sleeps over at a friend's house, ask yourself some key questions: Do you know the parents? Have you been to the home? Do you feel comfortable having your child at the home? If the answer to any of these questions is *no*, keep your child home until you can answer *yes*. And if one or both of the other child's parents make you uncomfortable or give you a "hinky" feeling, it's all right to say you have other plans or you don't feel your child is ready just yet.

If you do have concerns, have you talked to the inviting parents about them? Any honest, decent parent will understand when you say,

"Gosh, maybe I'm just paranoid, but I want my child to be safe. I'm sure you feel the same way." Ninety-nine times out of one hundred, the other parent will respond, "I totally understand. I feel the same way. Do you want to stick around for a while or have your child call before bed?" And feel free to say yes.

How to Prepare Your Child for a Sleepover

Before you allow your child to sleep over at a friend's house, talk to your child about how a sleepover is a big reward and a big responsibility. Tell your child that brushing his or her teeth is a public responsibility, because who wants to smell stinky breath in the morning? Remind your child that kindness and respect are required, and that he or she should always say please and thank you. You may have to have this discussion more than once.

Also, tell your child that doors should always be open, unless he or she is alone in the bathroom or changing clothes. Explain to your child that he or she should never be in a room alone with another adult when the door is closed. Then tell your child that if anyone does or says anything that is definitely wrong or does not feel right, it's okay to say no and to call home right away.

Peer Group Lesson #3: Expect and Address Public Discussions of Sex

Your child will encounter peers who have been exposed to the realities of sex and sexual behavior, whether it be through movies, television, the Internet, or a lack of supervision. Children who are exposed to this kind of information without the maturity or guidance to understand the complexity of the subject will usually do what all kids do: immediately go to school and tell all of their friends. This is not necessarily a red-flag behavior. In the vast majority of cases, the child who brings the sex talk to school has not been abused. The parents may not even know that their child has been exposed to the concept of sex.

If your child comes home from school with language, questions, or inappropriate talk about sex, call or meet with your child's teacher and discuss your concerns. If you're hesitant, think about it like this: If your child were the one talking about sex, wouldn't you want to know so you could address the matter immediately? While you may be inclined to think that this behavior is "natural," the classroom should be a sanctuary from "forced maturity," especially in elementary school. Your child and the other children in the classroom have the right to an age-appropriate school day. Your child's teacher will appreciate your concern and openness and will probably discuss possible actions and outcomes with you. Embrace the opportunity to help and partner with your child's teacher.

If the teacher does not confront the problem with compassion and action immediately, go to the administration for additional help. Teachers are not taught to deal with many of these issues in their graduate training, and younger teachers may need help, guidance, and input. I have worked with my son's teachers as a team to solve these kinds of problems, and we have had great success.

Do your best to ensure that any conversation with your child and your child's teacher about sex talk in the classroom emphasizes that there should be no shame. While using shame may be a quick way to stop sex talk in the classroom, it may also shut down children who are being sexually abused (whether now or later in life).

If the sex talk is happening at another child's home, approach the parent with the benefit of the doubt. The child in question may be getting information from older siblings or another child. Chances are that the parents will do their best to help their child and stop the behavior. If you get any pushback, or if the other parent thinks that sex talk at this age is not a problem, help your child find other playmates.

Peer Group Lesson #4: Forbid Playing behind Closed Doors

Insisting on no closed doors, except when a child is changing clothes or using the bathroom, is always a good rule. Your child should not be unfamiliar with this rule, especially since it's the law in many states that a child is never to be behind closed doors with a teacher or other adult in a school or church setting. Plus, you may have already discussed this with your child when it comes to visiting other homes (see lesson #2 earlier). So it won't be a huge stretch to tell your child that when he or she is playing with friends, doors must always be kept open.

If your child balks, make light of it and tell him or her it's because of the smell of "kid funk." But stick to your guns. Kids can get into enough trouble with doors open—they don't need the added temptation of shutting the door and keeping Mom and Dad in the dark.

Peer Group Lesson #5: Enforce the "No Secrets" Rule

The "no secrets" rule is not just for preschoolers. It should be the hard-and-fast rule for all children. Be sure to stress to your child that if anyone is being hurt or if an adult swears a child to secrecy, there is something very, very wrong and it is okay to tell you or a trusted adult.

Elementary school is the time when crushes blossom, especially for girls. By the third or fourth grade, your child may confide in a friend about a crush or be told about a crush that a friend has on someone else. These are totally harmless, and if experience is any guide, kids never keep those secrets anyway. If a child has an age-appropriate crush on another child, I consider that a "surprise" rather than a secret, since everyone finds out about it sooner or later and there is nothing harmful or malicious involved.

Red-Flag Behaviors among Peers

In addition to the lessons for parents on how to approach your child's relationship with peer groups, there are some red-flag behaviors that you should look for in your child's peer group. You should address these behaviors immediately, either with the parents of your child's peers or with your child's school.

Viewing, Discussing, or Possessing Pornography

Pornography, no matter the subject (child or adult) and no matter the medium (print or digital), is completely inappropriate for the five- to ten-year-old age group (and for ages eleven to eighteen too). If you see or hear about a child possessing any kind of pornography, immediately tell the child's parents. If the child has taken pornography to school, also address the subject tactfully and forcefully with teachers and/or administrators at your child's school. On the off chance the pornography was given to the child by a predator, the child's parents—and possibly the school—need to know immediately.

Abusive Behavior

Hitting, kicking, and biting, especially in the genitals, is never acceptable behavior. Yet it's all too common for a child at school or on the playground to decide that it's lots of fun to kick or punch other kids in the testicles. Do not turn a blind eye to this behavior. It is not only painful, but violent and inappropriate, and it can cause permanent damage. If your son is kicked or punched in the genitals, or if your daughter is hit or kicked between the legs or on her breasts, address the problem immediately. If the parents of the other child dismiss the behavior or say that it is "natural," make it perfectly clear that the child is not welcome to play near your child until the situation is remedied.

If this happens at school, go immediately to the administration. Your school should have zero-tolerance rules for this kind of behavior.

Playing "Doctor" or Nudity

Kids are curious beings. Playing the *I'll show you mine if you show me yours* game is a natural behavior and is not an automatic indicator of abuse or pathology. This does *not*, however, mean that you should allow it to happen around your child, whether on school grounds or in your home. If your child tells you that this behavior is going on, first acknowledge to your child that our bodies are interesting and different. Then say, "No one looks at or touches our naked bodies or our penis/vagina/breasts, etc." Tell your child that no one should ever be nude at school or while playing with friends—you can even make this funny by saying, "Ugh! No one wants to see *Mom* naked. Gross! So you shouldn't be naked at school or on the playground either." Laughter will get the point across.

If this is happening at school, report it immediately. Elementary school teachers are usually well versed in dealing with this issue. And be sure to follow up.

Bruising or Marks on Your Child or Another Child

Kids seem to attract bumps, bruises, and scratches. The more fun they have, the more marks show up on their bodies. But sometimes the marks are more than just simple knee-scrapes, and the injuries are bigger than a Band-Aid can handle. If your child or another child has marks that he or she will not or cannot explain, or cries about pain that he or she will not disclose, take the child to the doctor immediately. If a child tells you or your child that he or she has been beaten or injured by another adult or child, report immediately to law enforcement or call Childhelp at 1-800-4-A-CHILD. If you see or suspect sexual abuse, report it to law enforcement or an abuse hotline immediately. See chapter 8 on reporting abuse for more information on whom to call.

Remember, reporting is the right thing to do. It's not your job to investigate abuse, but it's your obligation to report it and get proper care for an abused child.

Threats and Bullying

If you suspect or see any signs of threats or bullying, whether face-to-face or over the Internet, address these behaviors immediately. Unfortunately, bullying is a real problem. Although this book does not address the complexities of bullying or cyberbullying, we've already discussed how this behavior is damaging and thrives on secrecy. Schools, homes, and playgrounds should be safe sanctuaries for children. Schools have zero-tolerance policies but often do not know there is an issue unless students and parents report.

If your child is being threatened or bullied by another child, take action immediately. Many schools have bullying reporting hotlines. Local police departments also have outreach officers that deal solely with bullying. Do your research now, and know the numbers to call in your area *before* the problem strikes.

Child-on-Child Sexual Abuse

Beyond threats, bullying, and other abusive behavior, in some instances a child will sexually abuse another child. Child-on-child sex abuse is real, and it is not uncommon. This is possibly the saddest and most heart-wrenching part of my work.

No one knows what makes a child a sex abuser. Sometimes the abuser him- or herself has been the victim of sexual abuse. The abuse "flips a switch" in the child's brain, and the child turns anger, rage, and shame into criminal behavior that may mirror his or her own experience. Scientific studies have shown that child sexual abuse can alter a child's brain development and chemistry, so it's not unrealistic to think that a child who has been horribly abused and does not get help might turn his or her anger toward another child.

Not all children who sexually abuse other children are victims themselves, however. Clinicians and researchers are trying to get to the root cause of this type of aggression, but right now we do not have all the answers. Still, we can teach our children to protect themselves and warn them that children can hurt them and must be reported. Child-on-child abuse is only now gaining attention, largely because kids are finally reporting and the police and the courts are taking action. These kinds of abusive crimes have been going on for time eternal, but as a society, we have not been willing to talk about it—or we have chalked it up to "playground bullying." Now that bullying is no longer considered "innocent," sexual aggression among children is finally coming into the spotlight.

Another reason we do not hear about child-on-child sexual violence is that our juvenile justice system—for good reason—protects the identities of juvenile offenders. Though you may not agree with this policy, it protects children who lack the maturity or decision-making skills to be held accountable for criminal behavior. Because of this, child-on-child cases usually remain sealed and are seldom, if ever, reported in the media.

A final reason we do not hear about child-on-child crimes is that we tell our children they should not tattle (a problem I also addressed in chapter 10). Kids who learn that tattling will be punished won't tell an adult when they see or hear another child being hurt in a school bathroom, in the neighborhood, or behind school buildings. Aggressive and abusive children reinforce this misguided policy; they are the first to say that no one likes a "snitch" or a "tattletale." While we would all like to think that our children are smart enough to know when to report, younger children are black-and-white thinkers. They do not know the subtlety of what an adult thinks is tattling or not. The solution is to encourage our children to be reporters. Help your child learn to problem-solve. Teach your child how to talk to adults when he or she is scared about things. Be sure to emphasize the idea that it is *always* safe to talk to you and that if another child threatens harm, it is even more important to come to Mom and Dad.

Your Child and the Internet

In our technology-driven society, children are exposed to the Internet at a young age. By the time your child enters elementary school, he or she is likely to be an intuitive master of Internet-enabled devices, but a seven-year-old does not have the decision-making skills to have complete responsibility over such devices. Chapters 12 and 13 go into more detail on Internet safety for older children, but here are things you can do right now to keep your five- to ten-year-old safer in cyberspace.

Internet Lesson #1: Know Every Internet-Enabled Device in Your Home

Look around at everything in your home that is "connected." These days, it's more than just computers and tablets; smartphones, iPods, iPads, Kindles, televisions, and video game consoles are all Internet-enabled, and the list is growing. You need to know every device in your home that is Internet-capable, and you need to know who is using it and where the users are browsing. Think about it like this: Would you let your elementary school-aged kid go somewhere in the physical world where you haven't been and don't know about? Then don't allow your child to go somewhere unknown in the virtual world.

Internet Lesson #2: Monitor, Monitor, Monitor

A seven-year-old does not have the decision-making skills to be given complete responsibility over an Internet-enabled device. Make it clear to your child that YOU own any and all Internet-capable devices that the child uses. Tell your child that since he or she lives in your home, you can and will monitor everything your child does on all devices. The younger the child is when you start this practice, the easier it will be to enforce.

Internet Lesson #3: No Devices in Bedrooms

This is a good practice for everyone to follow (for various reasons), but it is especially necessary for children. Internet predators gain access to children because children who are at home and in their bedrooms feel safe and secure and think that no one can hurt them. While your five- to ten-year-old may not be visiting websites (yet) that make him or her vulnerable to Internet predators, start a practice *now* that no Internet devices or video games should be used in the bedroom. As a bonus, this also will ensure that your child sleeps better, away from the temptation of texting, web-surfing, or late-night video games.

Internet Lesson #4: Restrict Multiplayer Games and Chat Rooms

A five- to ten-year-old doesn't need to play games with strangers on the Internet. Unless children are playing with a person they have met in person, they should not be in multiplayer mode on any Internet-enabled device. If your child is playing with someone he or she does know, still monitor the activity, especially if the other player is older.

Where do predators go? Where the kids are. Child predators love to hang out on websites for kids, because here they are surrounded by children and can even masquerade as a child. Even though you may trust the television programming on the Disney Channel or Nickelodeon, you cannot trust that anyone in a chat area on Disney's or Nickelodeon's websites is who they say they are. The best precaution: If you let your child play games online, do not allow him or her to enter any chat or group area that involves contact with other unknown users.

Internet Lesson #5: Put Restrictions on Devices

Make sure your child uses a password that only you know to visit websites or add games or apps to any devices. If you don't know how to block websites or apps, you can talk to a tech person who can show you how. While parental protections are not foolproof, they are better than nothing. Some devices, like the Google Chromebook laptop, will allow your child to go only on sites that you preapprove using another device. Do your research, and find the best devices for you and your family. Internet devices and gaming consoles vary, so read the instruction manual or talk to a tech expert to ensure that all of your Internet-enabled devices are secure. This will save you headaches and possibly hundreds of dollars in case your child decides to make dozens of in-app purchases for a game he or she installed on your phone.

* * *

I have worked with dozens of victims who told me the same story: *Mom and Dad let us run wild. There really wasn't any discipline in the house. We ran the roost. It seemed cool at the time, but I really wanted an adult I could rely on . . . I needed my parents to be parents. So, when I went to school, I didn't have any self-control. I got in trouble all the time. I ached for attention, whether positive or negative. That's when Mr. X started to take interest in me. He was that adult figure I had been looking for. He taught me things and listened to me. Soon, he was abusing me. And I couldn't tell my parents, because I knew they would blame themselves.*

Don't let your child say the same about his or her childhood. Take an interest in your child's peer groups, and be an engaged partner with his or her school and teachers. Be understanding yet firm as you help your young child adjust to life in the world outside your home.

Chapter 12

Who Is This Kid?
Getting to Know Your Preteen

One morning, you wake up and there is an alien in your house. This creature smells funny, speaks a language you don't understand, and constantly wants to get into border skirmishes with everyone else in your house. The creature sleeps long hours, has unpredictable moods (usually fluctuating from grouchy to silent), and seems to be constantly gripping and communicating on an electronic device.

Figuring out this creature is close to impossible until you see it among its peers. Then the creature who can barely crack a smile blossoms into a beautiful, funny, outgoing preteen. You barely know how to cope, let alone how to keep up with this creature's rapidly changing moods and needs.

And just yesterday, this creature was your beautiful ten-year-old son or daughter.

The Truth about Tweens

Preteenagers, or "tweens" (because they are wedged *between* early childhood and becoming teenagers), are dizzying, rapid-fire, dynamic, and beautiful. Their bodies are changing faster than their minds and moods can keep up. It's not an easy time for these kids. They are going through their biggest physical changes since the first two years of life. Their voices change. They grow hair. Their breasts and genitals start to look and act more and more like those of an adult. But these kids are still children, no matter how mature their bodies look and become.

Emotionally, they are a bigger mess. Hormones are raging in their bodies—tweaking their moods, creating and influencing menstrual cycles, and littering their bodies with acne. They can barely control how they feel and have no idea why their body acts and reacts the way it does, whether they are alone, among friends, or with someone of the opposite sex.

Tween brains are also going through rapid changes and developing into adulthood. Their decision-making processes may be blurred (or downright screwy), and often they lose the ability to focus. Academics, for example, may be thrown out the window—or may become the center of the child's life.

Girls who were once happy and free are now sullen and quiet. Boys who loved their mothers start to make the break and assert more independence. And since we are talking about tweens and how mixed up things are, the previous sentences can exchange the words *girls* and *boys* and still come out ringing true.

Even though you may hear your daughter tell you to leave her alone, she needs you more than ever. As much as your son believes that you don't understand, he aches for your guidance. This age group needs strong, loving, parental guidance and care more than ever, even though they are doing their best to push that guidance away. Tweens need mentors, teachers, and guides. They need their parents.

Picking up where chapter 11 left off, I am defining the "tween" period as generally between ages eleven and fourteen. But these numbers are not hard and fast. Your middle school–aged child is a unique and beautiful creature who may physically and hormonally develop earlier or later than his or her peers. And those two might not happen together: Some kids may experience the emotional and hormonal issue but not physically develop until much later, while others experience the opposite. Whatever your tween's path, it's a schedule over which he or she has little control. Be flexible, listen, and use compassion. Your relationship with your tween may save him or her from falling prey to abuse.

Why Are Tweens So Vulnerable to Predators?

Predators love this age group. The more successful a tween is in pushing away his or her parents, the more vulnerable that child is to grooming and sexual abuse.

Anytime there is great change and instability in a person's life, that person is vulnerable to predators—not just sexual predators, but also financial swindlers and other con artists. The changes a person undergoes can be physical, like puberty. They can be external changes, like a divorce, a move, or a job change. They can be emotional, like a health diagnosis, a death in the family, or other personal loss. But unlike adults, your eleven- to fourteen-year-old lacks the brain development, life experience, and maturity to identify many of the bad people who want to cause harm.

Think of how vulnerable you would be if you lost your major source of income tomorrow. Now imagine how you would handle the situation if you were twelve. For twelve-year-olds, many of life's traumas are as painful and as devastating as a job loss is to an adult. The more you understand and appreciate the sheer intensity with which tweens live, the more you will be able to comprehend how and why your tween reacts to situations the way he or she does. *Everything* in your tween's life is earth-shattering, from a crush on a pop star to being excluded from a clique to rejection by a sports team or academic program. And because your tween can't sort through the intensity and chaos of emotions, he or she is inclined to overreact to situations you may consider benign. This is the age where we start to see serious depression, eating disorders, and suicides. So while you may consider your twelve-year-old a total drama queen (or king), cut your child some slack. Tweens can't help it. Try to empathize so you can help your tween solve issues before they become problems and so you can armor him or her against predators.

Unfortunately, predators already know exactly how to relate to this group. They know how to embrace tweens and convince them that their parents are wrong and unfair. They know tweens' moods and how to placate them. They know that boys cannot control their physical reaction to sexual stimuli. They know how to isolate a boy, flatter him, and then make his body respond, even if the boy is scared, isolated, and resistant. They know that girls at this age fall in love "quick and hard." They know that it's easy to turn a girl's desire to be a woman against her and to groom her for abuse. They know the power of secrets and sexuality.

And these predators are not only men. As we've explored already, women can and do abuse, and while female predators seldom target prepubescent children, their numbers increase dramatically as children age and mature through puberty. By being aware, we can stop all predators, no matter their gender.

Your Tween and Sexual Identity

I have worked with many sexual abuse survivors who wonder whether same-sex abuse (a man abusing a boy or woman abusing a girl) is the reason he or she grew up to be homosexual. Many others who identify as straight are scared or ashamed because they believe that perhaps deep down, they may be gay. Let me put these fears and misconceptions to rest.

Predators are smart, and they are cunning. They want to find the most vulnerable victims, so they spend years practicing: grooming children and finding the most compliant victims. When you look at the tween demographic and all of the changes that the eleven- to fourteen-year-old is going through, who do you think might be the most vulnerable in this group? Usually it's the children *who feel as though they are different from their peers*. Who are the kids who usually feel the most isolated from their peers and also often have fewer resources and guidance? Tweens who are struggling with their sexual identity or growing into the understanding that they are homosexual. Predators zero in on these kids because they know how vulnerable and impressionable they are—even more so than most tweens. Most of the time, these kids don't even understand why they feel the way they do. Many times, they don't have the words (or are simply too scared) to tell their parents or another trusted adult about their feelings. Predators, on the other hand, know exactly how to act and what to say to these kids.

Does this mean that all same-sex abusers target only children with sexual identity issues? No. There are other ways a kid in this age group can feel "different" from his or her peers. I have worked with child sex abuse victims who were groomed because their predator helped them deal with acne, a serious injury, or the simple fact that they were taller or smaller than their peers. Predators also love to target the children of alcoholic or drug-addicted parents, because a tween is just beginning to understand the real problem. They love to target kids whose parents are going through divorce or who have recently moved away from their familiar circle of friends and family. They love the kid who is lonely, whether the child is physically isolated from peers, emotionally isolated from family, or internally isolated from the world.

Even the most poised kid—someone who looks and acts the right way and says all of the right things—may feel lost, alone, and totally isolated, especially as a tween. This chapter will help you raise a tween who is a "hard target" and is not isolated and vulnerable.

Self-Esteem: A Predator's "Kryptonite"

Ask any victim of child sexual abuse what could have protected him or her from being vulnerable, and that person is likely to say, "Self-esteem." Like the radioactive material that sapped Superman's power, a deep-seated sense of self undermines a predator's tactics and has repelled many a would-be abuser.

Don't confuse *self-esteem* with *self-confidence*. As we discussed in chapter 2, self-confidence is when kids *act* (and most of the time, feel) as though they have their act together. Self-confident kids are pleasant, outgoing, popular, and poised. Self-esteem, on the other hand, is when the kid likes him- or herself and *feels* proud, happy, and content with who he or she is, how much he or she is loved, and his or her potential and power. Sometimes the kid who acts in a confident way is the one who is wracked with the most self-loathing. And a predator will see that right away.

So how do you help your middle school–aged child build a deeper foundation of self-esteem? Let your child explore and find things that spark his or her interest and ignite his or her passion. It could be sports, martial arts, a club, performing arts, music, gaming, photography, a job, church activities, a subject in school, or love of animals. Help your child find a hobby he or she loves and is good at—one where your child can teach, mentor, continue learning, or present. Not every child will find a passion at a young age, but learning, loving, and being good at an activity is the best way to cultivate inner self-love and self-esteem—a major deterrent for predators.

Tackling "The Talk"

Puberty is the most obvious symptom of this age period, though really it's an umbrella full of symptoms. Your son may grow by a foot or may not grow at all. Your daughter may have been in a bra and menstruating since age nine; other girls may not need a bra until mid–high school. But whether you can see it or not, their bodies are changing. And you need to be ahead of the game.

Just as we empowered our children when they were toddlers by teaching them the correct names for their body parts, we need to be sure that children of this age begin to understand their bodies and know how they function. Girls need to know about menstruation, hygiene, and why it's important that they keep their bodies clean. Boys need to know that erections and wet dreams are natural, healthy, and not shameful—and need to be warned that erections at the wrong time (math class, anyone?) may be embarrassing, but are simply a fact of life. It's also appropriate to have a discussion about masturbation so they know this is a natural way to explore their bodies—something that can feel good but should be done alone, in private. Both girls and boys at this age are old enough for "The Talk" about how babies are made. Your child's reaction at this age may be "Why would anyone ever want to do *that*? Yuck!" But as long as your tween has this information from you, another adult cannot twist it or use it for his or her own advantage.

Perhaps you think your son or daughter is not "mature" enough to handle The Talk yet. Well, I would like you to think about something: Mary Kay Letourneau began sexually abusing Vili Fualaau when he was twelve. His parents may have thought he was too emotionally immature for The Talk, but his sixth-grade teacher got to him first. And though he was surely a child emotionally and mentally, he was physically old enough to father a child. The Talk is necessary at this age, and it needs to go beyond simple mechanics.

What Do I Tell My Child about Sex?

How you choose to couch the discussion of sex with your preteen is up to you. Your family may insist on virginity until marriage. Or you may take a different approach: *If I can't stop teens from having sex, then I will be sure that they are protected.* No matter your position on this topic, you need to armor your middle school–aged child against sexual abuse.

Here are some things that you can tell your tween *now*—things that can help *before* your child gets into a situation where an adult may try to groom or molest him or her.

- Adults should never have sex with children. Period. It's against the law for a reason. It can hurt and damage you more than you can even begin to understand. That means teachers, coaches, or anyone with power over you.

- If an adult ever says it's okay for you to be sexual with them, they are lying and taking advantage of you.

- If an adult tries to be sexual with you or talk about sex with you, it's not because you are mature or an adult. It's because they want to take advantage of you. The reason they want to have sex with you is because you are a child, and they are predators. Once the victim becomes an adult, the predator will lose interest and move on to another child.

- If you ever hear about an adult—a coach, teacher, priest, elder, family member, or anyone else—having sexual relations with a child or trying to have a sexual relationship with a child, come tell me immediately.

- A predator—and it may be someone you love and care about very much—will try to tell you that sex is "fun" or that masturbation is a "release" that two people can do together. These are lies. Anyone who truly loves a child will never be sexual with them.

- Predators know that kids your age think about sex a lot. They also know that there are a lot of things that you are too grossed out about to talk over with your parents. If there is something that you need to talk about, please tell me or (our trusted adult). Never confide in someone who will use it to take advantage of you.

- It's really hard to be your age. I know. I was your age once. And while things are different now, many aspects are exactly the same. But if you trust me enough, I can help you. If I can't help you, we can find someone who can. You are never alone.

Adult Body, Child Mind

Tweens are physically maturing as their bodies morph from child to young adult. But an adult body does not equal an adult mind. While most people think of this age group being vulnerable to men, this is where we begin to see more and more female predators. Because some boys may look like men at fourteen and do not have control over their bodies' responses, they are especially vulnerable to adult women who feel it is okay to "break in" young boys.

There is *no such thing* as "breaking in" young boys to sex. If an adult woman has sex with a boy, it is abuse, even if the boy has the physical response of erection and ejaculation. Just because the boy's body responded does not mean that his mind or emotions understood or wanted the encounter or that he could comprehend the damage it would cause.

You will find yourself looking at certain thirteen- and fourteen-year-olds and cringing at their "adult-looking" bodies. Many kids this age will dress to match that new physical maturity, which will probably upset you even more. Remember, no matter how old a child looks, he or she still has the mind and mentality of a child. Never put mature-looking or -acting children into situations they cannot handle, such as adult parties or bars.

It is perfectly okay to discuss your child's choice of clothing if you believe it is inappropriate. While no rape victim "asks for it" by wearing or not wearing some item of clothing, do your best to let your child know that he or she can never control the actions of other people. Let your child know that attracting unwanted attention may not garner the outcome your child is looking for. And yes, it is fine and right for you to tell your eleven- to fourteen-year-old that he or she is not allowed to dress in ways that are revealing or provocative.

It's a point that bears repeating: No child deserves to be sexually abused because of the way he or she acts or is dressed. A girl who is sexually abused at fourteen is not guilty of "asking for it" because her skirt was "too short" or she "acted so mature." But a well-armored child—one who has had The Talk with a parent and is aware of the risk that can accompany certain choices—will take steps to avoid problems in the first place.

Depression and Behavioral Issues

Depression is a real problem in this age group. While some tweens may be considered moody, others suffer from real and damaging depression. Suicide, unfortunately, is not uncommon in this age group, and kids who are dealing with identity issues, bullying, abuse, or problems in the home are even more vulnerable.

If you think your child is depressed, get help. In many cases, kids can't just "snap out of it," and your intervention can help save a kid's life.

What does this have to do with abuse? Depressed kids need help, guidance, and a way out of their pain. Predators know this, and they supply victims with drugs, alcohol, or the attention that the child craves.

Children with other behavioral issues (ADD, ADHD, etc.) are also vulnerable. For many of these kids, life and school are a struggle, and positive attention from an adult is one thing that they crave. Make sure that if your child has any behavioral issues, the positive attention and love he or she gets from adults comes from you and other trusted adults.

Communicating with Your Tween

This is definitely the age where you will, as they say, attract more flies with honey than with vinegar. In other words, being dogmatic, authoritarian, and rigid with your tween will probably result only in anger, defiance, and rebellion. And an angry, defiant, and rebellious kid is a target for predators.

I am not suggesting that you instantly turn into a softy or throw all the rules out the window. In fact, considering the added responsibilities and freedoms, your tween should face more rules than ever. But how you pass down those rules—your delivery—can make all the difference.

What do I mean? I have worked with hundreds of victims whose abuse started when they were between the ages of eleven and fourteen. Victims in this age group carry a great deal of shame that victims who were abused at a younger age do not. Why? Survivors who were victimized at a younger age tend to see themselves more as innocent children who lacked the power or authority to do anything to stop the abuse. Tween victims, however, have a tendency to feel they had a choice in the abuse. They think they had the power to refuse or repel their abuser. Thus they can be unforgiving—not of their predator, but of themselves.

Why the dramatic difference? When kids hit age eleven or so, they tend to think of themselves as more mature and adult; they see themselves as having the ability to make important decisions, even though they are still children. This is biology's way of preparing young bodies for adulthood, whether adulthood is becoming president of the United

States or hunting with the caveman clan. But all the bravado of this age group does not hide one important thing: These kids are still children, still vulnerable, and still in need of parental guidance.

Listen, Validate, Guide, Mentor

In public relations and marketing, big campaigns or promotions always consider various "stakeholder" groups. A stakeholder is someone who is directly affected by the promotion or campaign but who typically is not a decision-maker. When a decision is to be made, stakeholders have the satisfaction of knowing that their concerns and needs will be heard and validated. Stakeholders may not make final decisions, but they have an influence. They are important because their adoption and acceptance of the campaign is vital to its success.

Your tween, with his or her budding mind and growing body, is a stakeholder in your home. He or she has opinions, values, and ideas that should be heard and respected. Does your tween make final decisions? No. But if you listen, ask questions, respond with care, and offer alternative suggestions, your child will feel as though he or she is a valid and important member of the family. Your "no" answer, when it comes, will not seem as authoritarian, "unfair," "mean," or "out of touch." Not everyone is happy, but everyone feels as though they were treated with respect. Even a child who is mad about your refusal will know that he or she got a fair shake and won't look to another adult for validation.

Listening to and validating your tween's input—in other words, treating him or her like a stakeholder—is a key method that predators use to gain a child's trust and confidence. Kids want to be treated with respect, even though they don't have the tools or understanding to comprehend many of the issues your family faces. Instead of the predator filling this role, you as a parent need to be the one listening to and validating your tween.

The other two things your child needs at this age—and a predator knows this—are guidance and mentorship. That is why so many predators work and volunteer as coaches, teachers, clergy, camp counselors, and Boy Scout leaders. These positions give predators not only access to kids, but the *right kind* of access—the kind where a predator can be a mentor and a guide. A predator knows that with the right words and the right guidance, he or she can create a compliant victim. By listening, giving advice, and mentoring a child through the maze of middle school, he or she will gain that child's implicit trust.

How do you block that? Mentor and guide your child at home. Pay attention to the adults in your child's life, and make sure that anyone else who is mentoring your child is a trusted adult—not someone who will use your child's willingness to learn and desire to be validated as an excuse to molest him or her. Guide your child through these difficult, tumultuous years with a balance of limited freedom and careful attention. Fill your child's heart and soul at home so your child won't attract a predator who will gladly take on that role.

Predators look for the weak spots in your child's armor. With the eleven-to-fourteen age group, as with the fifteen-to-eighteen age group we'll discuss in chapter 13, your ears and your mouth will be the most valuable tools you have to armor your child against abuse.

The Role of Love

Predators have a powerful tool—one more powerful than money, gifts, promises, or opportunity. In fact, they know this one tool can get a preteen to do anything the predator wants . . . and do it with compliance. That tool is love.

It's a twisted and convoluted love, because the child may be scared, confused, alone, or under the influence. But in the eyes and heart of a preteen, it is a real and powerful love. That's what makes this abuse so tragic.

Survivors are reticent to talk about this dynamic, because some adults misunderstand and use this idea of love to find another reason to blame the victim for what happened. Defense lawyers capitalize on it, because if they can show that the child willingly showed up at the predator's door, they can poke holes in a court case and help a child molester go free.

But predators *make* children fall in love with them. When targeting the eleven- to fourteen-year-old (and all the way to age eighteen), predators use their skills, honed over decades of grooming and abuse, to get children to love them, no matter how terrible the abuse. This is why children and teens continue to go back to the predator's home, class, or other space, even though they are scared, confused, hurt, or isolated.

More tragically, it's why kids do not report and why, when confronted with allegations of abuse, they will often defend the predator. This is also why cases of incest are so tragic: The child is "in love" with the predator, who is supposed to be a source of unconditional family love.

How do you stop this cycle? Make your family a "hard target" by providing a home life that is not remote and chaotic, but full of honest and unconditional love, openness, and support. Take notice of a change in your child that goes beyond the typically bizarre tween behavior. Is your child becoming isolated and withdrawn from friends and family? If so, open up the lines of communication once more, and send plenty of love your child's way. Go back and review chapter 4 on predatory grooming behaviors. It is perfectly age appropriate to discuss red-flag behaviors from adults and peers with your tween. In fact, talking about grooming with this age group can open up many discussions with your child about their world outside of your home.

Finally, if you meet a survivor, be compassionate about this dynamic. Never ask victims why they "kept going back" to the predator, why they didn't tell their parents, or why they may have defended the predator. We all know love is a complicated emotion, especially for the young— and it's even more so when it's entangled with abuse.

Your Tween and Hazing

Believe it or not, hazing is an ugly truth of many sports and clubs in this age group, not just later in high school and college. What is hazing? It's a peer group–focused initiation into clubs, sports teams, activities, sororities and fraternities, or societies that involves harmful or dangerous activities. Hazing can include drinking alcohol, beatings, lack of sleep, verbal abuse, dares such as water intoxication, dangerous driving, playing dangerous sports without safety equipment, overexertion by exercise, and in a few occasions, sexual abuse.

Why sexual abuse in hazing? Remember, sexual abuse is a crime of power, not a crime of sex. There is no better or more horrific way to show complete power over a new member of a team or club than to degrade them through sexual abuse. The practice at the high school level is far more common than is reported in the media. Kids *want* to be members of these sports teams and organizations. They are afraid to report because they fear that they will be blackballed and that the team or club (which usually has strong support by parents and administrators) will be disbanded.

In all cases, hazing is inappropriate and possibly illegal. If you or your child hears of hazing in a club, school activity, or sport, report it immediately to school or team administrators. If the behavior is abusive, violent, harmful, or criminal, report it to law enforcement. No child should ever be hurt, abused, or sexually molested as an initiation into a high school club. If the club or team is disbanded, don't feel guilty. What is more important: a winning record or the safety of the children on the team?

Your Tween and the Internet

We have discussed how predators capitalize on a tween's daily struggles: low self-esteem, issues at home, need for love and attention, concerns about body development, desire to be treated as an "adult," isolation from family and peers. Predators also use pornography, sex talk, "secrets," "deep friendship," an "us versus them" mentality, promises of fame and success, and overnight trips away from family and friends. Grooming over the Internet happens in much the same way, and the expanding role of the Internet in our children's lives makes this a crucial area of focus when armoring your tween against risk of abuse.

The Internet rules and lessons for younger children (see chapter 11) still hold for preteens, so let's revisit them here. If your child is on social media, the biggest rule you can offer is this: If you do not know a "friend" in real life, then do not "friend" that person on any kind of social media. Parents also need to carefully monitor their tween's usage, track all accounts (and make sure their child doesn't have secret accounts), and constantly remind their child that everything sent over the Internet can affect his or her chances at college and jobs. In fact, there are numerous articles about companies and colleges hiring "social media scouts" whose only job is to track what applicants do online. Sharing those articles with your child may be helpful.

Tell your child *never* to give personal information to anyone over the Internet—not his or her address, phone number, school, or current location. If you pitch this to your child as *It's just not cool* rather than a *You had better* never *do something like that*, you are more likely to get buy-in.

Avert problems by making sure that all technology is kept in family spaces and no Internet-connected devices are allowed in the bedroom. If you get pushback, tell your child it's a hard-and-fast rule for everyone in the house who is under eighteen. (And consider making it a hard-and-fast rule for the adults too. Bedrooms are great places to designate as "technology-free" zones.)

If you decide you want robust Internet tracking on all the devices in your home, inexpensive software programs offer varying levels of monitoring. Warning everyone in the house that you are installing the program should remove any temptation for your child to venture into chat rooms or go on websites that you do not preapprove. It may seem a bit draconian to slap monitoring software on your computers, however, so if you prefer, you can work from a position of trust and the honor system. Either way, the easiest way to remove temptation is to keep all computers in family spaces.

Smartphones and Handheld Devices

Technology is getting smaller and smaller—and more and more affordable. Smartphones that just a few years ago were too expensive for most adults are commonly seen in the hands of middle schoolers today. This amounts to putting predator access in the palm of your child's hand, with no parental guidance or limitations.

There is only one quick and clean answer to the problem of smartphones and kids: Don't let your kids have them. Ask any Internet sex crimes investigator, and he or she will agree. This may make you the least popular parent in the universe, but it is a real and viable option. Phone companies understand that some parents do not want their kids to have smartphones, and some companies manufacture phones that only make calls and allow texting. Deciding this is a good option for you will not only remove much of a predator's access, but also save you money, reduce temptation, and save your child's eyesight.

Regardless of what kind of phone you may allow your tween to have, you need to make and keep strong family rules about its usage. As technology changes, these rules will likely need to be adapted, but here is a good start on phone rules for an eleven- to fourteen-year-old:

- All phone calls, photos, and texts can and will be monitored.

- No password-protected apps or phones, unless parents have the passwords.

- No phones in bedrooms.
- No apps without prior approval.

Of course, you can add more restrictive rules, such as limiting the number of texts, the call minutes allowed, or the hours during which the phone can be used. Most important, however, is to be consistent and apply punishment as appropriate. Going over a minute allotment because your child needs help on a science project is an understandable offense. Texting at two a.m. is not.

Apps and Social Media

Do your best to keep up with the latest apps and social media sites. This may be almost impossible; even the experts have a hard time keeping up. But if you keep good lines of communication open with your tween, it will be easier to learn about the latest websites and apps that can lead to trouble. The best way to prevent problems is to know and require approval for every program and app on your child's devices. If you need more help, local and national law enforcement agencies can bring presenters to your child's school, community group, church, or club. Agents give presentations to parents about the latest in Internet safety and how to spot online predators. More important, they can also give age-appropriate presentations to kids and show the "true faces" behind online friends, avatars, chat buddies, and fellow gamers who target children.

Anonymity and Online Sexuality

People will do and say things on the Internet that they would never do or say in real life. Adults will be hateful, act like bullies, divulge secrets, and take naked pictures of themselves and send them to peers and potential lovers. Unfortunately, teens and preteens are not much different. Girls as young as eleven or twelve are sending nude or semi-nude photos of themselves to boys because they see celebrities do it, or because they believe that because they took the picture alone, in their bedroom or bathroom, it is a "private" moment. This is a scary, sad reality.

There is a set of truly innocent victims here as well. If a child sends nude, seminude, or sexualized photos to a girl or boy who does not want the photos or has no idea that the photos are coming, the receiving child is now open to punishment, scrutiny, or possible criminal charges, depending on the degree of sexuality in the photos. To help avoid this, make it clear to your child that you monitor the phone, including text messages, photos, and app usage. Encourage your child to tell his or her friends how strict you are about this—your tween will probably be happy to complain about it!

Parenting Tools: The Three Rs

Understanding and communicating with a tween can be challenging and exhausting. Validate your child's opinion and emotions, but do not rely on your child to be your confidant, counselor, or sounding board. Instead, your role should include three special tools for dealing with tweens: relationships (family and friendships alike), rules, and respect.

Relationships

Relationships are the key to this age group. The more you can guide your child to create healthy and dynamic relationships with his or her peers, the more you can help your child create healthy relationships through life.

As we discussed earlier, your child's model for healthy adult relationships begins with you. Teach your child through example what proper emotional and physical boundaries are with adults. Your child hears, sees, and absorbs everything. You want positive, affirming, and loving input from you to affect your child's relationships.

Use this time to show your child how to build family bonds through fun. If you have children of varying ages, create "compromise" activities that get everyone involved: things like family game night, lifelong sports (ski, golf, camping, hiking, biking), and community or church activities. This is also a great opportunity to include a friend of your child's in your family activities. Create the space where your child looks to you and your family as partners in forming positive relationships with other adults and peers.

You may be doing "everything right" when it comes to being open, loving, firm, and compassionate with your kid. Even your best intentions, however, can be derailed by a bully at large or a friendship gone sour. Ninety-nine percent of your young teen's friendships are neutral or positive, but the remaining 1 percent can cause lasting damage. The way to mitigate that damage is to remain active in and inquisitive about your child's social life.

School relationships also loom large. This is the start of the period in your child's life where bullies and "mean girls" can devastate his or her self-esteem. You cannot micromanage your child's day at school or hold your child's hand as he or she grapples with peer group problems. But you can do things to help your child problem-solve his or her issues. If your child experiences a problem that needs to be addressed at school, encourage him or her to address it with teachers and administrators.

Despite all these other relationships, your child's attitude, school success, self-esteem, and potential for getting into trouble will be determined by the power and influence (good or bad) of the peer group. Know who belongs to this group and what they stand for or are known for.

Finally, if you feel that your child is truly suffering, don't say, "Be tough. This too will pass." Sometimes it does not pass. If switching schools, finding other educational options, or changing or dropping out of activities can help your child solve some of his or her traumatizing social issues, help your child make the best decisions.

Rules

This may sound crazy to you, but your child *wants* you to make the rules. Rules and boundaries make a tween feel secure and stable—your tween knows exactly where he or she stands and what is expected. Your child doesn't want you to give him things because you feel guilty about your parenting. Your child can see right through that empty tactic.

We all have our moments of parent guilt. You may work too many hours, be a divorced or single parent, introduce step- or half-siblings into the home, or feel as though you cannot provide what you should for your child. Do not try to make up for it by parenting with guilt. Don't feel bad for limiting your tween's Internet time because you only see him every other weekend. Don't give your tween an expensive smartphone because you feel bad that she has to share a home with step-siblings. Don't allow your child to be rude or disrespectful to you because you feel bad about yourself.

Guilt is not a parenting tool. Be an adult. Be a parent. Be a strong guide and mentor with lots of love, real compassion, and strong rules.

Respect

Respect is the most important lesson for this age group. You want your child to respect and depend on you, not on a predator. Teach your eleven- to fourteen-year-old to have true respect for you and your role as parent and guide; respect for other trusted adults, teachers, leaders, and mentors; respect for peers; and respect for the challenges, difficulties, and successes they will face.

The discussion of respect can start with being polite—looking adults in the eye, speaking to adults and peers without sarcasm, and taking other people's feelings and opinions into account. Also show your child the importance of *self*-respect: treating him- or herself with compassion and grace. Encourage your tween to look at situations from other points of view. Ask your tween how teachers, friends, adults, and other people feel when he or she acts or speaks a certain way. Most important, teach your child that happiness does not come from money, social stature, or geography any more than it comes from being "cool," putting other people down, or hurting anyone. True self-worth comes from a place of respect: a combination of compassion, love, and a positive attitude.

*   *   *

No one—least of all tweens themselves—is quite sure what's going on in their minds and bodies. But when you truly engage with your child and get involved in his or her guidance, you can face both the highs and the lows of the tween years as a parent, not a friend. The more empowerment and careful guidance you can give your child, the less likely your child will become a victim—of predators, of depression, or of life.

Chapter 13

When Communication Counts: Talking to Your Teen

They act big and brave. They think they are invulnerable. But inside, they often feel like a fraud. And their brains? Underdeveloped, over-stimulated, and exhausted. Welcome to being a teenager.

Close your eyes and think back to your time at high school. Forget that you have teenage children now, or that you may have watched your siblings go through four years of high-intensity social and academic rigor. Think about yourself. What were your teen years like? If you're like most of us, high school comprised the four most influential years in your life. That's not to say that those years are the be-all and end-all, or that the years between fourteen to eighteen are the most *important* in a person's life. They are not. But when you look at influence measured by intensity, relationships, and social "status," no time is more influential on a person than the four years of high school—the crucial years your teenager is going through right now.

Turning Lessons into Strategies

The healthiest among us take the high school experience, grow from it, and develop into well-adjusted adults who understand that life is *not* defined by what you did or who you were in high school. But for the vulnerable teen who becomes the abused teen, these four years can be devastating—and the devastation extends throughout the victim's entire social circle, who can be just as hurt, isolated, and confused by what an abusive teacher or coach did to their friend.

Emotional pain felt during these years can be far more intense than pain experienced in the years before or after, and entire communities can be destroyed when a predator targets a teen. So this chapter is important not only for the parents of the vulnerable teen who may be targeted for abuse, but also for teens who carry the burden of a friend's pain, who may need to report and who may even have witnessed abuse. It also speaks to other adults who need to understand that although a teen may look and act like a "grown-up," he or she is still vulnerable to cunning predators who hope that all blame for the abuse will sit squarely on the teen.

There is a lot of overlap between this group and the younger tweens we discussed in the previous chapter, so consider reading both if your child is anywhere between ten and eighteen. The more you can understand and comprehend the wide ranges in maturity, responsibility, and development among teens and preteens, the better equipped you will be to understand and prevent abuse.

This chapter is an especially important one to me. My own sexual abuse began when I was fifteen years old. Although I was vulnerable because of my home situation (my mother was an alcoholic and my father lived in a perpetual state of denial about the effect of his wife on his two daughters), I was the "perfect" kid. I was smart, savvy, and funny; got straight As in school; and by all accounts, was a kid who "had my head on straight." I didn't drink, do drugs, or act out sexually. When my abuse began, I had "made out" with boys, but all we ever did was kiss. I was adamant that I was going to stay a virgin until I was married.

How could a kid like this get so off track? It was easy: I had no trusted adults to guide me or mentor me. No one taught me how to make decisions. And when I chose wrong, I was shamed. It's no wonder a predator seized the opportunity.

I also had the misfortune to attend a high school that was rife with abuse in the 1970s, '80s, and '90s. There were few to no boundaries between teachers and students, and it was not uncommon for dozens of boys to watch movies, swim, and hang out at the unmarried principal's house. And of course, rumor has it, the boys were sworn to secrecy about drinking alcohol there.

The abuse at the school was almost cartoonish in its prevalence and abundance. But the awful lessons that my peers and I learned have been transformed into the preventive strategies outlined in this chapter. We were a bunch of good kids who were exploited. But because we survived, I am able to use our stories to show you how to raise a well-armored high schooler.

Most of the tools I discuss in this chapter involve bringing up ideas and issues with your teen before he or she is faced with potentially scary or confusing situations in real life. A predator's power is in the element of surprise. I'm not saying a predator will jump out of a bush to nab your teen; instead he or she will present situations that your teen does not know how to get out of or how to combat. But you can undercut a predator's efforts by talking directly and honestly with your teen and then *listening to his or her feedback*. When you consistently discuss problems and issues your teen may face—and teach him or her how to say no—your teen will be better armored than the majority of teens out there. Together you will create that all-important hard target that predators will avoid.

Your Nemesis: The Teen Brain

You have already survived the pain of your child's tween years. You have faced the moodiness, the hormones, the tears, the disappointments, the anger, the crushes, the bullies, the anguish—and yes, the joy. Hopefully, both you and your teen made it through relatively unscathed. But now you have an even more formidable foe: your teenager's brain.

By the time your child is fourteen years old, there have been numerous moments when your kid has done something that you (and the world at large) consider to be extremely stupid, careless, reckless, or incomprehensible. You know what I am talking about—those decisions your kid makes that make you want to wrap your fingers around his or her neck and scream, "What were you thinking?"

Even more maddening is your kid's answer: "Gee, Mom, I don't know."

Here's the rub: Most of the time, your teenager is not making a lame excuse to cover up his flawed logic behind why he broke the window/totaled the car/neglected to turn in homework for a month/ let a friend keep his rat in your garage without telling you. There is a good chance that your teenager does *not* know why he or she makes those decisions.

Even more frustrating is that even when your child *knows* there are serious consequences and risks to decisions like throwing a party without permission, driving too fast, pulling a prank, or sneaking out of the house, he or she will still do the wrong and dumb thing. Why? Their brains are wired that way.

Daniel J. Siegel, a clinical professor of psychiatry at UCLA and author of the excellent and engaging book *Brainstorm*, is an expert on the chemistry and development of the teenage brain. His thesis is that teenagers make nonsensical and risky decisions because *they are biologically wired that way*. While he goes into great detail about the hows and whys, we can narrow it down to three things you need to know as a parent:

1. Although a teen's body may be at its peak physical strength, his or her brain is not yet fully developed.

2. Teenagers make risky decisions not out of rebellion, but because they are attracted to and intrigued by the risk (even when they know the outcome will most likely be bad).

3. Your teenager needs tons of sleep. Period.

Teens love risk. They drive too fast, go on scary roller-coaster rides, try drugs and alcohol, complete dares, and push the envelope in every possible way. Is this because of the way these particular kids were raised? If your child does risky things, have you failed as a parent? No. It's a part of the biology of their brains.

Go back fifteen thousand years—or look at the world's remaining tribal and native cultures that have not been exposed to modern technology—and you will see that the teenage boys are warriors, hunters, and "in your face" alpha men. And it's not because they are the smartest or the most strategic. It's because they will run into battle or face a mother bear defending her cubs, even when they know death is a real possibility.

Is this an evolutionary survival mechanism or a lucky stroke of nature? Scientists are still figuring that out. But the next time you watch a war movie or read about the latest real-life military skirmishes, take a look at the men at the front lines; although in many societies women are not allowed in combat, their brains are wired the same way. It's the youngest—the eighteen- and nineteen-year-olds—who are sent into battle. Why? Because they will run in, head-first, with a devil-may-care attitude. Armies seldom win wars when they fill the front lines with men and women in their early to mid-thirties. If they did, the charging line would look at the foe, turn to the battlefield commander, and say, "Maybe we can just talk this whole thing out."

The military's gain is a parent's loss. The wiring that tells a warrior it's a good idea to storm a building full of insurgents is the same wiring that tells a teenage boy it's okay to accept pornography and alcohol from a trusted coach. The same impulse that makes soldiers run across battlefields also tells teenage girls that it's fine to go to their teacher's house alone.

We need to teach our teens to take a breath, think it over, and say no, which may defy their very nature. It's not easy, but the first and most effective step is the easiest: having conversations about decision-making.

For decades, parents responded to their teenagers' dumb decisions with anger, frustration, and punishments. Considering they didn't have the tools and understanding to know why their kid was acting that way, the response was pretty reasonable. Yet it only made things worse. A parent's intense, emotional reaction puts the teen on the defensive, and a hurting, angry teen often becomes even more rebellious.

Does your teen need to be given boundaries and appropriate punishments for inappropriate behavior? You better believe it. But this book asks you to take a breath before you react, and reminds you to do much more talking and much less yelling. For a confused teen—the kid whose favorite answer to everything is *I don't know*—the more you can provide information and help, the more likely he or she will be to listen.

Your teen is not going to change overnight. In fact, much of the behavior that frustrates you will not change at all. But if you address decision-making when your teen is still young, explaining how the teen brain is wired and how to make good decisions despite that—you can give your kid a great advantage, both against abuse and in life generally. When your teenager knows he or she is fighting a battle against a brain that can't keep up, that child is more likely to recognize bad decisions and people who are trying to take advantage.

Communicate, Communicate, Communicate

Parenting is a lot about habits. You do your child's laundry every week (or several times a week!). You take your child to school, sports, and other events. You keep up on vaccinations and buy new shoes monthly for your child's constantly growing feet. Now there is another habit for you to adopt: communication.

This entire book has focused on the importance of verbal and non-verbal communication with your child. From the time your child was a baby, you have been asking open-ended questions, modeling positive behaviors, doing your best to communicate without anger or judgment, and maintaining strength and consistency.

Now you have to kick it up a notch.

Not only do you need to ensure that you are properly communicating with your teen, but now more than ever you need to be a guide and mentor. You must teach your child how to communicate with peers and adults in uncomfortable and awkward situations, how to act responsibly when there is trouble, and how to say no with grace . . . and mean it.

Your teen may not be talking much, but he or she wants you to listen. Teens generally run hot and cold when it comes to talking. You know how it is—you get nothing but annoyed grunts and exasperated moans at the dinner table, but thirty minutes later, when you are busy doing something else, your teen comes to you and wants to talk. It's going to be hard, but you need to focus on the end goal. Don't miss the boat when your child is willing to open the lines of communication. Turn off everything: no computers, no smartphones, no television. If your teenager wants to talk, you need to *listen*.

Teenagers don't want to hear a lecture, and they don't want to listen to anyone drone on and on about how insignificant teenage problems are. They want a mentor and a sounding board. They want you to see that their own ideas have merit, even as they're asking you (perhaps indirectly) for guidance.

Good mentors guide their mentees to their own conclusions. They don't hand down decrees. Try to talk to your teen the same way—starting with the honest-to-goodness truth.

The Value of Truth

Do you like it when people lie to you? Do you appreciate it when you are not given complete information or are left in the dark? Of course not. Neither does your teen. In fact, although teens can be experts at stretching the truth to save their own hides, they have a tremendous amount of respect for truthfulness in others.

Truth should come with discretion, however. Your child does not need to know about your sex life (trust me, your child *doesn't want to know*). Don't trouble your teen with the issues you're facing on the job or in your marriage, or with anything that can be construed as a burden or stressful. Your job is to use relevant and age-appropriate truth to help your child solve problems. And your kid will appreciate your candor.

An example of how the truth can help is with teenage pregnancy. Parents of an older generation felt that a teenage pregnancy was a source of shame and should be kept secret. My mother didn't tell me about her own teenage pregnancy until I was twenty years old, although she had told my older sister when my sister was thirteen. The reason, she said, was that she didn't think I was mature enough to handle that kind of information. My sister took the lesson to heart and understood that sex had serious consequences. But by the time my mother told me, it was already too late. The power of the lesson was in the truth and in my mother's willingness to be open and honest with my sister.

Discretion is key. Many parents have parts of their life that they do not want to revisit, especially with teenagers. Others may have episodes that have been kept from spouses. Don't "out" other people, and don't disclose what you are not ready to embrace about yourself. But if there is a part of your life that is full of lessons your teen might appreciate, share them. Anything you can do that is honest, age-appropriate, and genuine will help engage your teen. The result? He or she may become more honest and genuine with you in return.

Be Available

Teens who are struggling with grooming, abuse, or other issues need your strength, even when they don't have the words to tell you so. By being there and being available, however, you express nonverbally that your teen can rely on you. Sometimes "being there" is just sitting next to your teen while he or she watches television, does homework, or plays video games. You don't have to interact particularly, so it's not a matter of being "intrusive." It's about sharing the same space, with respect for each other. For a teen, that proximity without demand—the fact that you enjoy sharing the same air as your teen without asking for anything in return—can help your teen understand that you are a support system, close by when you are needed and available even when times are not rough.

Talking to your teen about sex and sexual abuse is much more complex than in "the old days," when our society thought that teens (male or female) could not be molested by women, that only homosexual boys were molested by men, and that girls who were fifteen and sexually abused had "asked for it." Considering all this, it's a challenge we should welcome.

Hopefully, you and your teen have already talked about abuse and how adults target kids. You have talked about the warning signs of grooming and about the proper boundaries between teenagers and adults. Now that your teen is older, you can go into greater depth about the damage that abuse causes and about the stereotypes that kept victims quiet for decades.

If you are uncomfortable or embarrassed to talk about sex, get over it. You felt the same way about teaching your toddler the proper words for genitalia, and look how well that turned out! As before, you will not be talking about anything worthy of embarrassment or shame. By talking about the facts of life, you will be empowering your teenager. So put on your "big boy pants" and start the discussion. Being available and communicating life's truths to your teen are surefire ways to offer greater protection against harm.

Teaching Your Teen to Say No

Predators who target teens know the best ways to get what they want are to isolate the teen from his or her peers and to blur the line between what the teen knows to be right and wrong. They create situations in which the teen doesn't know how to say no, despite the bad feeling in his or her gut. Of course, completely ignoring their gut in the first place is just what teenagers do when they take risks. So a predator's job becomes easy.

Teens, unlike younger kids, are no longer concrete thinkers who look at the world in terms of black and white. They love to use their new understanding of subtlety, innuendo, relativism, and nuance to debate parents, influence peers, and justify increasingly stupid decisions. You need to immediately address your teen's failing ability to use reason. You need to teach your teen how to again see things as concrete and in terms of "right and wrong" so peers and potential predators cannot get the better of him or her.

The Power of Peer and Predator

Think about how powerful a peer group is. Even a strong, smart kid can be convinced to do almost anything—stay out past curfew, vandalize a building, drink, and use drugs—if the peer group surrounding the teen is persistent and convincing enough. In fact, your teen will go directly against gut feelings if peers can convince him or her that "everyone else is doing it."

Now think about how convincing a predator is. Men and women who want to exploit a child for sex have probably convinced even themselves that what they are doing isn't wrong, telling themselves, "This teenager is smart enough and old enough to handle it." Predators minimize their crimes at every opportunity and do their best to confuse the situation, shift blame, and try to portray the child as a "willing instigator" of the abuse. With younger victims, this is tough to do. The child may always blame him- or herself for the abuse, but parents, police, and prosecutors will never believe that a boy in a Little League uniform or a girl playing with Barbie dolls was intentionally asking for sex. So predators have to use other ways to minimize the abuse in this age group, like calling the abuse "love," saying the child is lying, trying to pass off the abuse as misunderstood horseplay, or confusing the child about what happened.

With teens, there are countless opportunities to get the victim right to the predator's front door and to blame the victim for abuse. Teens are mobile. They are given responsibilities in other areas of their lives. They date their peers. They are obsessed with sex. All these things make it easier for a predator to access potential teenaged abuse victims—and create a string of situations that require a teen to say no repeatedly to an adult they probably admire.

In my own abuse and the abuse of dozens of other survivors with whom I have worked, there was always that "seminal moment" in the grooming process—that *one situation* where, had we just said no, we could have been spared a future of abuse. This situation can be a camping trip, an indulgence in alcohol, an invitation to the predator's home, a late-night party, a school function, or some other event. It's the moment we replay in our heads, telling ourselves, "I should have listened to my gut."

Am I blaming myself or other victims for the abuse we suffered? No. I am saying we didn't know how to say no to that *one* question or statement that made us a target. Maybe it was *Do you want to come and see my new car?* Or perhaps it was *Gee, you are really mature for your age. It's so easy to talk to you.* It could even have been something as simple as *Close the door. I want us to have some privacy.* We didn't know how to refuse potentially "hinky" situations. We trusted that all adults—even if they did or said things that made us feel odd—had our best interests at heart. We were risk-taking kids who were already targeted because we lacked strong adult role models, lacked self-esteem, or were dealing with chaos in our lives that the predator was able to calm.

And we couldn't say no.

The Most Important Word in Your Teen's Vocabulary

When your child was three, *no!* was his or her favorite word. To armor your teenager against abuse, you need to remind him or her to use it—and maybe even *how* to use it.

Close your eyes and think back again to when you were a teenager. If you got into trouble, what did you do? With whom did you get into trouble? Were you a ringleader? Were you a follower? Did you do things you may have regretted because you wanted to fit in or be accepted? When you did get in trouble, what was the number one thing you could have done to avoid the problem altogether? While you keep thinking, I'll give you a hint: It's also the number one thing you can teach your teen to help him or her ward off a predator. It's the power of listening to one's gut and saying no.

The goal in teaching your child how to say no is helping your child get out of an uncomfortable situation with grace and free from blame. You don't want your child to be ridiculed by her peers, so you will need to create a "bad guy" who can take the heat off—someone who can take the blame for your teen's refusal, giving your teen the breathing room to make a decision without worrying about being booted from the peer group.

The bad guy is you.

Talk to your teen about potential situations that he or she may face when out with friends. Acknowledge that there will be invitations to parties where there will be drinking, drugs, or other issues. Recognize that he or she may be invited on late-night joy rides where kids may be drunk. Introduce the idea that your teen may be in a situation where his or her peers are engaging in criminal behavior. Ask your teen what he or she would do in any of these situations. Would he or she go along? What if there were no other way to get home? What if your child really liked one of the people involved and wanted to impress that person? What should your teen say when faced with the power of both predator and peer?

Tell your teen to make you the bad guy. Come up with potential excuses your teen can use to avoid dangerous situations and also avoid ridicule or pressure from peers. Suggest that your teen say things like, "I can't afford to get in trouble again. I'll lose my car/ be grounded for months/be pulled off the track team." Work out strategies with your teen, and formulate options together. Both you and your teen know that saying, "My mom will get mad," will not convince a bunch of risk-charged teens. So work with your teenager to see what will be effective.

Giving the Predator a Reason to Pass By

What does teaching your kid to say no to peers have to do with sexual abuse? Everything. I discussed the "seminal moment," that one decision a teen makes that can change the course of grooming and abuse. Vulnerable teens are seldom prepared for verbal manipulation from a cunning adult who wants something from them. But armed with the ability to say no, your child becomes a hard target.

Predators don't want the battle of the conquest. They want to find the easiest target to groom and molest: the child who does not report, the preteen who is groomed into compliance, and the teenager who doesn't know how to say no. If your teen says no even once to a predator, chances are that the predator will move on, unfortunately to an easier target. While we don't want anyone else to be abused, naturally you want your child to be the kid the predator "passes on."

Although this lesson is also important for younger teens (as we saw in chapter 12), a fourteen- to seventeen-year-old has a great deal more freedom than the younger teen. He or she is able to get places by him- or herself, whether that means staying later at school, going in early to work, or volunteering at the local nonprofit. A predator can convince a boy to come in early to work to provide extra help, or can beg a girl to stay late at the food kitchen for a heart-to-heart talk.

And the only thing that can stop them is your teen saying, "No."

Prepare your teenaged child to say no to an adult in these situations just as you prepare him or her to say no to peers. Talk to your teenager about potential situations. No employee should need to go in to work early if he or she is not being paid or the boss does not have a good reason. Let your child know that he or she doesn't have to be alone or stay late at school, a volunteer location, or a sports practice.

Be frank with your teen: If your child has a crush on an adult who is paying special attention, he or she needs to step back and think. Tell your teen that an adult who is safe and trusted would never be alone with a child in an isolated or sexually charged situation. And be sure to tell your child that a safe adult would never put anyone at risk of abuse. Explain all this as soon as possible, and don't underestimate your child's maturity or his or her need for this information. Warning your child before the crush can stop the crush from happening altogether.

This approach to empowering your teen has a lot in common with the top lessons for toddlers (in chapter 10)—in particular, allowing a toddler to say no to the adult hug or kiss. By telling your teen that it is okay to say no—even if he or she fears losing a job, a grade, or a position at a volunteer organization—you are giving your teen tools to stop abuse and identify grooming behaviors. By saying no with respect and confidence, your teen will let predators and others know that he or she is a hard target and cannot be threatened or coerced into doing anything that is wrong, immoral, hurtful, or inappropriate.

These lessons will not happen by osmosis. Your teen won't just "absorb" good decision-making skills because you and your family do your best to model them. Your teen will need practice, discussion, and feedback to actively *learn* the skills of saying no and making firm, safe decisions. And you want your child to learn these skills from you now, before he or she heads out into the wider world.

Do Natural Leaders Still Need to Learn This?

Bullies and natural leaders have one thing in common: They rely on their peers to validate their decisions, actions, and leadership. Bullies use threats and violence—whether verbal, physical, or emotional. Natural leaders do it through positive actions—they lead by encouragement, good example, and a positive attitude. But these leaders still need to learn how to stand up to those in positions of power and say no.

Because bullies thrive on attention and accolades, they are extremely vulnerable to predators who flatter them. Predators are more than willing to provide that flattery to gain access to the bully and to everyone that the bully dominates. So, reinforce the power of saying no and listening to your gut with your teen, even if he or she stands out as a leader. Whether your child is a wallflower or the class president, a homeschooled scholar or a schoolyard socialite, he or she needs to learn how to say no respectfully to adults and peers.

New Freedoms, Responsibilities, and Opportunities

Because high school may be the center of your child's academic and social life, if he or she encounters sexual abuse during this time, chances are that it will happen at school or at an activity connected to school. Plus, your now-mobile teen may also have a part-time job or engage in volunteer work. Your teen is busier and encounters more adults than ever . . . and you are seeing less and less of him or her.

Remember, predators go where the kids go. If a predator likes smaller children, he or she will go to places that offer access to them; the same goes for older children and teens. So as your teen's world expands beyond both home and school, new freedoms arrive alongside new responsibilities. The result may be opportunities for success and for damaging scenarios, both of which are explored below.

Dating

At the start of high school, your child may be going to formal dances in a group with friends. Even a child who is not permitted to date until age sixteen or seventeen may have a "steady" boyfriend or girlfriend that he or she sees only at school or church—a special friend who takes up all of your teen's time on the phone or the Internet. Or perhaps you allow your shy seventeen-year-old son to take a girl to dinner or to a movie—"just as friends," of course. Dating is a set of stages, and each child and family must navigate their own path through. Having a frank discussion can help with some of the "sticky stuff" that can get in the way of two teens enjoying each other's company.

Premarital sex or sex between teenagers of the same age is a personal discussion involving private decisions that must be left to the teen and the parents, and so it is not the subject of this book. But here are some things you will want to discuss with your teen as you address the issue of healthy relationships and sex.

Physical or Emotional Abuse

Explain to your child what constitutes physical or emotional abuse. Talk to your teen about put-downs, shaming, or pressure about sex. Tell your teen that abuse does not follow stereotypes and that a girl who hits or degrades a boy is just as damaging as a boy who does the same to a girl; the same holds for partners in same-sex relationships. Tell your teen that he or she deserves better than that type of treatment, and that if anyone your teen is dating tries to hurt him or her, the only safe option is to walk the other way.

If your teen is in a relationship where there is a deep emotional bond and trust, the other person may disclose abuse to your child. Tell your teen that reporting is not a betrayal and that if the other child is in danger, you and your family can provide a safe haven.

Sexual Activity in the Home

When an adult allows teen sexual activity in the home, it is a cause for concern. This can be an effective grooming technique for predators who specialize in teens. By allowing teenagers to have sexual contact with each other in his or her home, a predator is normalizing sex and making it easier to blur lines with a potential victim. Tell your teen to be on guard against any adult who says that he or she welcomes sexual behavior in the home.

Sexting

Sexting and sending nude photos via text message or the Internet is *not* a part of a loving relationship between teenagers. While this behavior may seem normal to your teen because movie stars and celebrities do it, it is dangerous. Your teen may believe that he or she can trust the recipient of such messages to the moon and back, but all bets are off after a breakup. Furthermore, what if someone else were to get ahold of the Internet device and send the photos to hundreds of other people, including porn sites?

Tell your teen daughter that if her boyfriend wants nude photos, he may not be the loving person she thinks he is. Tell your son that if a girl on the Internet asks for a nude picture, the person asking is most likely *not* a girl. Make it clear that you monitor all Internet devices and that her picture can end up anywhere—with your teen's name on it. The same porn sites that carry pictures of girls also carry pictures of boys—with all identifying information included.

If your teen has concerns that a friend will send nude photos to him or her, tell your child to announce to anyone who will listen that his or her mother regularly monitors the phone.

Jobs

A part-time, after-school job can be the ticket to financial independence and responsibility that you and your teen have been craving. Jobs teach teens the value of money and a strong work ethic, help a teen find out what career may be right for him or her, and provide valuable life experience. A part-time job also puts a little extra cash in a teen's pocket to save for college, a car, or other things a teen wants to have or do.

Sexual Harassment at Work

The vast majority of your teen's experiences in a part-time job will be positive. But unfortunately, sexual abuse of teens on the job is a problem that companies and parents face anytime a child under eighteen is employed. I have worked with teens who have been sexually harassed and abused on the job at national coffee-shop chains, at mom-and-pop stores, and as summer camp counselors. Typically in these situations, an adult in a position of power uses that power to groom or coerce a working teen into sexual activity. Predators love working in organizations where they have access to teenage employees, because the employers look at these kinds of cases as sexual harassment rather than child sex abuse. Also, teens who are sexually abused at work are even less inclined to report, not only because of the shame of the abuse, but because of the mistaken notion that a crime happening at work is a regular part of the "adult world." The teen also may be afraid that reporting the abuse will lead to losing his or her job and being "blackballed" for future jobs. Coworkers are also less likely to report this kind of abuse out of the same fears of losing jobs and future prospects.

Large corporations pay big money for insurance and legal costs to protect themselves against child sex abuse litigation. Even one case going to trial can sully the reputation of a national or international company. In smaller companies, each employee constitutes a big monetary investment in time and training, and a sex abuse lawsuit can be devastating.

Most sexual harassment and sexual abuse on the job happens because teens are not aware that it can happen, that it is a crime, and that they can do things to stop it. When I had my first "real" job, no one told me that I would have to fend off one of the adult managers who was well known for trying to "pick up on" the teenaged help. Had someone told me it was safe and okay to turn to him and say, "Stop it," I could have saved myself a lot of hassle. Instead I pretended that I didn't notice and that his attention didn't bother me. I was afraid that if I stood up to him or reported him, he would fire me.

Tell your teen that if anyone tries to take advantage of him or her, the only solution is to tell the offender to stop immediately. If the offender doesn't stop, tell your teen to immediately report the behavior to his or her supervisor, or to the police if the behavior is criminal. Your teen should take notes or create a log of every instance of harassment or attempted abuse and who witnessed it. Let your teen try to document this on his or her own first. If nothing happens, or if your child is minimized or threatened by company management, go in with your child to meet with a supervisor. If the action does not stop, give your teen the power to quit the job without shame.

Adult Parties

Adult parties and similar situations associated with the job are by far the predator's favorite way to get special access to teens. If your teen is working at a job surrounded by adults, like at a restaurant or coffee shop, he or she will be invited to adult parties and get-togethers. If there is alcohol or drugs, it will be easy for a predator to "normalize" this behavior and offer some to your teen. These kinds of parties also blur other boundaries, including sex. Now your teen will have his or her guard down, will be surrounded by adults, and will be a ripe and open target for abuse.

It is perfectly fine to restrict your teen from any work party that is not an "official" work-related activity. You can remind your teen that most adults do not want to "party" with kids because of the vast differences in maturity. In fact, point out that any thirty-year-old who wants to "party" with a sixteen-year-old is not the kind of person that other thirty-year-olds want to be around.

You may get pushback, but this is where you have to stand firm and be consistent. High school parties are challenging enough for a teen. Don't allow your child to be thrown into adult situations with no adult defenses.

Disclosing Grooming and Abuse

Unfortunately, you cannot control whether or not your child's friends are abused or exposed to abuse. And chances are that if your child has a good friend who has been sexually abused, that friend will trust your child enough to disclose to him or her. This is another situation you want to address before it happens. You don't want your teen sworn to secrecy by his or her best friend, or threatened by a predator who doesn't want your child to disclose what he or she knows. I am not exaggerating here. Both of these things happened in my own case.

Nor do you want your child to report to school authorities alone, especially when the school may already know about the abuse and be in the process of covering it up. And you especially don't want your child to carry the burden of witnessing a friend being hurt—or to feel the ultimate betrayal that happens when the friend "chooses" to remain in the abusive situation with the predator instead of accepting your child's help. Teens who are being sexually abused have a hard time breaking free from their predator, even when they have the full support of their friends. Don't let your child face this alone. Talk about the nature of abuse, show your child how to report, and discuss why it is important that your child always come to you with what he or she knows.

In the discussion of mandatory reporting (chapter 8), I pointed out the importance of reporting abuse as a crime, not as a personnel issue or a minor dispute. This means you need to make it clear to your child that if he or she hears anything about abuse, reporting it is both a duty and an obligation. Tell your teen that reporting protects the victim, helps earlier victims, and saves potential future victims from abuse. You may have to give your teen several examples of what to say. Prepare him or her for potentially serious pushback, including being the possible focus of a lot of anger from the teen who is disclosing. But if you can show your teen that he or she is not alone and is doing the right thing, your child will be strong enough to come to you and report.

Also prepare your teen to recognize the signs of grooming (which were introduced in chapter 4). A teen who understands it is wrong for an adult to give unwarranted flattery, gifts, alcohol, money, or porn, or to engage in sexually charged behavior with anyone under age eighteen, will be able to spot grooming among her his or peers. A teen who is informed about what grooming is and why it works will be far less susceptible to its influence.

Tell your teen it is okay to come to you and talk if he or she sees instances of grooming among peers or feels as though he or she is being groomed. Think of your child's journey through the teen years as a roadmap. The end of the journey is adulthood, with its freedoms and responsibilities. The key to being a success and entering adulthood lies in your teen's ability to pass certain milestones, to read the map for him- or herself, and to make the right decisions on the journey. You may not even know many of the adults that your child reports to in these situations.

If you give your child options and skills for how to address the roadblocks and hazards he or she will face, your child is far less likely to be abused or fall prey to a predator's grooming.

Drugs and Alcohol

This book does not go into all of the issues, temptations, and consequences your teen will face when it comes to drugs and alcohol. But I will say this: Drugs and alcohol are a predator's best friend. Many sexually abused teens I have worked with got their first taste of drugs or alcohol from their abuser.

If you or your teen's other caregivers are heavy drinkers or drug users, you can figure that your teen is not oblivious. Teens may even use it as an excuse to drink and use themselves, so look at your own usage and solve your personal addiction issues. A predator who knows you are a heavy drinker or user may use it to convince your teen that it's a "cool" or "adult" thing to do.

Talk to your teen honestly about drugs and alcohol. Let your teen know that there are serious consequences—legal, physical, and at home—if he or she uses either. It is far easier to abuse, molest, or rape a drunk or high person than it is to abuse, molest, or rape a sober person.

Tell your teen to be a hard target by refusing to drink or do drugs, in any situation.

Your teen may balk and say, "My friends would never let anything happen to me." Be sure to tell your teen that when people are under the influence, they make bad decisions, have poor reflexes, and allow things to happen that they would never condone if they were sober. It's not the job of your teen's friends to take care of him or her. And chances are, they will do a pretty lousy job.

Here at last is an opportunity to take your teen's cell phone—the one that I have continually urged you to monitor, the one that is glued to your teen's hip—and put it to excellent use. If your teen has a smartphone, make sure there is a taxi or ride share app on it, and make sure the apps are connected to a valid credit card, so if your teen is stuck and needs a ride, he or she can get home even without any cash.

Tell your teen that he or she can always call you for a ride, and that you will do your best to never be judgmental or fly off the handle if you receive a call asking for help. Make it perfectly clear that if your teen calls you because he or she is drunk and does not want to drive—or has tried drugs and is scared—you will be fair. What you want to avoid at all costs is for your teen to drive drunk or accept a ride from someone who is drunk or suffering from an overdose or adverse reaction to a drug. Make sure that your teen knows that if a situation can end badly, the best answer is always no.

Travel

Times have changed in the past few decades. Teens are traveling all over the world with performance groups, sports teams, and language clubs, and are even living abroad as exchange students. Unfortunately, sexual abuse can be a big problem in these situations. The best way to prevent it is to armor your child against the danger he or she may face abroad.

If your child is traveling, ask about some of the risks he or she might face. Ask your child why the countries he or she is visiting may be more dangerous than your hometown. Discuss drinking laws. Talk about being a hard target and avoiding drugs and alcohol, even if the legal drinking age is lower in the country he or she is visiting.

Also, be honest with your teen about stereotypes about Western teenagers. Let your teen know that predators in foreign countries may view Americans (especially teenage girls) as sex objects or consider them to be "easy." Reinforce the fact that when leaving the home country, your child needs to be mindful and respectful of the laws and customs where he or she is going. In fact, like any guest, your teen should probably be extra careful. In many other countries, the "rules" that your teen has relied on do not apply.

Tell your teen to be cautious, polite, and assertive. Remind him or her not to be foolhardy or take needless risks.

Work with your teen to gather all the emergency consulate numbers in the countries he or she will be visiting and to make sure that the numbers are stored in a safe, easily accessible place. In case of sexual assault or another crime, your teen needs to call the embassy or consulate and the local police.

And finally, make it perfectly clear that there is an entire breed of predator that focuses only on foreign tourists—even the ones who think they "know it all." Remaining in public, open spaces, and relying on polite and strong assertiveness will be your teen's keys to success.

Mentors versus Pied Pipers

You know who the "pied piper" at your kid's school is: the charismatic leader described in chapter 6—the teacher or coach whom all the teens love. This is the teacher who "gets" kids, or the priest who "really understands what it's like to be a teenager." The pied piper's classroom or office is always full of kids, and there is usually a hierarchy, with one child being the "most special" and garnering the most attention.

Most of the adults your teen will encounter are good people who know and respect boundaries. Responsible adult leaders who maintain proper boundaries will make sure doors are open at all times, will never be alone with teens, and will never allow discussions to veer into sexualized subjects. The responsible adult never has teens to his or her home unless it is a sanctioned event with other adults in attendance. The adult with proper boundaries always makes sure that parents are well informed and that there is no room for second-guessing his or her actions or intentions.

This is about the other kind of adult: the one who takes his or her popularity with teens and turns it into an opportunity to groom and molest.

A great example of this predatory pied piper is drama teacher Lynn Seibel, mentioned in chapter 6. Seibel was the "cool" teacher at his exclusive Minnesota boarding school—the guy whom students could confide in. He answered their questions about sex. He condoned their drinking in the dorms. He even let them have "naked dance parties" in dorm shower rooms. His classroom was constantly filled with teens. When he became a dorm parent and moved into the same building as the boys, it was normal to see him enter boys' rooms, especially if they were talking about sex or his favorite topic: how to enlarge their penises. The boys loved to be around Professor Seibel. So when he began to molest them, no one said a word. In fact, in a sworn deposition, Seibel himself said that he used his poise and personality to manipulate his victims so they kept coming back.

Beware the Pied Piper

Here are some red flags that you should immediately discuss with your teen and address with the adult whose behavior matches that of the pied piper.

First, a teacher, coach, or other adult should not invite your teen alone to movies or other activities. Of course, there are many trusted organizations such as Big Brothers/Big Sisters where an adult volunteer will spend time with a teen in a mentoring situation. These volunteers are usually carefully screened, although screening does not weed out all offenders. Parents should be cautious and ask questions anytime an adult spends long periods of time one-on-one with a teen.

If an adult wants to mentor your teen, speak honestly with the adult and find ways that your teen can be mentored in situations that are safe and not isolated from parents or friends. If the adult just wants to "hang out" with your teen, insist that you join them. If this makes the adult uncomfortable, then carefully consider the adult's intentions. An adult should not ask a teen to spend time alone together after practices or events. If the adult is giving your teen a ride home, insist that the adult bring the teen straight home; also, there must always be a third person in the car.

Second, there is never a good reason that an adult should invite a kid to stay overnight at his or her house. Only peers should ask your teen to spend the night. If it is a matter of convenience—for example, your teen needs to get up early for a game or track meet—be prepared to get up early and take your teen yourself. The invitation may be innocent, but why take the risk?

Third, be wary of any adult who becomes defensive about your concerns for your child's safety. Don't worry about hurting feelings. An adult who says that "no other parents have had an issue" or that you are being "too overprotective" is not to be trusted anyway. Remember, you are not restricting your teen from spending appropriate time with his or her peers. If an adult truly wants to spend time with your teen, that adult should be willing to do it in safe, open, and transparent ways.

Finally, be wary of the adult who is always surrounded by teens. Back in the "old days," parents used to love and admire the adult who was surrounded by groups of teenagers. Perhaps these parents didn't know how to relate to their kids and were impressed that someone else did. Other parents were just happy to get a sullen teen out of the house and into something that interested him or her. Whatever you do, don't think that another, more popular adult will solve your issues with your teenager. Only you—and time—can do that.

Most of the time, the adult who is surrounded by teens is just an adult who enjoys the company of teenagers. But even then, is that the kind of role model you want for your teen?

Mentors Insist on Transparency

You want your child surrounded by transparency. If there is a positive adult mentor in your child's life, here are the behaviors you should expect:

- An adult mentor will always say it is okay for parents to be a part of any activity.

- An adult mentor will always meet with your child in your home or in open, public spaces.

- An adult mentor will never act in a secretive manner and will never ask for privacy with your child.

- An adult mentor should never text or email your child late at night.

- An adult mentor should never try to get between you and your child.

- An adult mentor should have meaningful discussions with both you and your child.

Proper adult mentorship can be a positive, life-changing experience for a teen. But only if you take active steps to ensure your child's safety.

Signs of Sexual Abuse in Teenagers

Teens are at risk of a double dose of danger when it comes to abuse and the symptoms of abuse. Teens who are currently being abused will show signs and symptoms. But the teenage years, rife with hormones, growth, brain development, and mood changes, are also when many children who were abused at a younger age will begin to show signs and symptoms. This is because as a teen matures, he or she will begin to understand that the abuse of years earlier was wrong. But because of emotional immaturity, the teen may not be able to express the pain, understand that the abuse was not his or her fault, or get rid of the self-loathing and shame.

If you see any signs of sexual abuse in teenagers, talk to your teen and seek help. Some of the signs listed here can also be symptoms of a bigger psychological problem that must be addressed immediately:

- Cutting or other self-injury
- Depression or bipolar behavior
- Anger and rage issues
- Bloody clothing or underwear
- Isolation from peers and family
- Secretiveness
- Sudden changes in mood (a previously happy child is now always sullen, or an even-keeled child is suddenly full of rage)
- Fixation on a certain adult
- Talk about suicide or violence
- Quitting favorite activities for unexplained reasons
- Dropping out of school unexpectedly

- Hiding dirty clothes
- Body shame
- Serious weight gain or anorexia and other eating disorders
- Destruction of well-loved books, sports equipment, or musical instruments
- Abusive behavior toward other teens or smaller children

Sticking your head in the sand and pretending that your child is mature enough and smart enough to stay out of harm's way is not going to work. Your teenager needs guidance and lessons in following the gut and saying no in uncomfortable situations. A teenager with a plan is a safer, stronger teenager.

You may not even know many of the adults that your child reports to or associates with in these situations. But if you give your child options and skills for addressing roadblocks and hazards, he or she is far less likely to be abused or to fall prey to a predator's grooming.

Chapter 14

Child No More: Sending Your Young Adult into the World Safely

Throughout this book I refer to your "child," and that will not change in this chapter. But these are not children we are talking about anymore. While you will always refer to your son or daughter as your "child," this chapter addresses a relationship that is developing between two adults, even though one of those adults (you) may still be in a position of emotional and financial power.

As an adult, your son or daughter will come to understand their responsibilities to themselves and to society; as a parent, you must transform your role too. Depending on your relationship with your child—Are you paying for college? Does your child still live at home? Is your child in the military?—you will also need to grow and mature in how you communicate.

You still have much to give, and your child still has much to learn. The key to keeping your child safe in the world without you by his or her side resides in your ability to effectively communicate your input and concerns while not seeming condescending or patronizing.

Talking with Your Young Adult

We all know that not everything you discuss with your child will stick, but when you talk about these subjects and show that you care, your child may remember that he or she made a promise to be accountable and may think more carefully about all kinds of decisions.

Here are some things to tell your young adult:

- *It is time to be an adult, act like an adult, and make adult decisions.* The law sees your child differently after age eighteen. Let your child know that this is his or her big chance— a huge opportunity that comes with responsibility and accountability.

- *Follow your gut.* Teach your child to think like a "risk assessment officer." Let your child know that he or she will walk into situations thinking, *Nothing good can come of this.* In those situations, it's okay to turn around and walk away. Your child should also look out for others and help keep friends out of harm's way. It's also okay for your child to ask his or her peers to be accountable as well, especially if they are a part of an organization.

- *Sexual assault does not discriminate between men and women.* Remind both sons and daughters that sexual assault can happen to anyone. Don't let your son believe that he cannot be a victim of rape.

- *Rape is not about sexuality, it's about power.* Reinforce this fact as many times as you need to; it bears repeating.

- *Think smart and take precautions at all times to become a hard target.* Have honest talks about alcohol and drugs and the role they play in sexual assault—for both the predator and the victim. While no victim ever deserves to be raped, a drunk or high person is a much easier target than a sober one.

As always, most important of all is to make it clear to your child that you will always love and support him or her no matter what. Teens and young adults have a tendency to made poor decisions, and as long as you make it clear that you are there to help and guide, your child will be more likely to come to you when he or she needs help.

Reporting Sexual Assault

After high school graduation, no matter what the next steps are for your child or what community he or she joins—college, military, work, travel, or something else—your adult child is likely to encounter sexual harassment or assault in some way. Make sure your child knows how to report sex crimes in each of these situations.

On Campus

If your child or someone he or she knows is the victim of a sex crime on campus or at another location, call the police. If they tell you to call the campus police force, tell them that you want an officer from the local police there as well. Demand it.

We know that colleges and universities, like churches, sports teams, and clubs, are *not* in the business of investigating sexual assaults, whether they are committed against children or adults. University committees and policies are not organized to investigate or prosecute crimes, and they do not protect the rights and dignity of either the accused or the accuser.

Tell your son or daughter to have the number for the local police handy and to always call 911 in case of emergencies. After calling 911, your child should contact RAINN, the Rape, Abuse, and Incest National Network, which offers a twenty-four-hour rape crisis line at 800-656-HOPE and help online at RAINN.org. Encourage your son or daughter to make sure friends follow the same procedure.

In the Military

If your young adult or someone he or she knows is sexually assaulted on a military base, encourage your child to immediately notify the military police—local police have no jurisdiction on military bases. If the assault happens off base, even if the crime is committed by a fellow serviceman or -woman, urge your child to call the local police and 911 in addition to calling the military police.

The Rape, Abuse, and Incest National Network, in conjunction with the Department of Defense, also provides a twenty-four-hour hotline for male and female victims of sexual assault in the military, at 877-995-5247. You can find more information at RAINN.org.

Traveling to a New Place

If a sex crime is committed in a foreign country, tell your child to call the twenty-four-hour US Embassy hotline for that country. He or she should then call the local police if it is safe to do so. It is always a good idea to have these numbers handy whenever you or your child is traveling outside the country.

If your child is traveling within the United States, be sure to point out beforehand that the United States is a large country with diverse laws and customs. What is okay at home may not be okay three thousand miles away, even if you are still in the US. Being understanding and respectful of laws and customs can go a long way to helping your young adult stay out of trouble.

*   *   *

The scariest thing after sending your child to high school is sending your child off to college or the big wide world. Make sure you prepare your adult child to seek out and know the resources that are available in the case of any sexual crime or harassment. Knowing these numbers and procedures beforehand could make all the difference should your child need to act quickly in a dangerous situation.

College Life—and All That Comes With It

That inevitable moment has finally arrived—the moment when your seventeen- or eighteen-year-old graduates from high school and makes the decision to leave home, whether it be for a trade school, a job, a four-year college, or the military. But that doesn't mean your child will be leaving behind the risk of sexual predators. Sexual assault in all of these settings is a problem—and on a college campus perhaps most of all. And it's a problem with no answers at the moment.

There are no real statistics on campus sexual assault. We know only that sex crimes are underreported—and that colleges and universities have a horrible track record of reporting crimes. All you can do is be prepared and prepare your child for the risks—and then hope for the best. If you have armored your growing child every step of the way, your college student will know what to do and how to avoid risky situations, protect him- or herself, look out for friends, and report sexual crimes.

Alcohol and Drugs

The problems of alcohol and drugs, which we addressed in the previous chapter, only increase in college. Binge drinking and drunkenness greatly increase the chances of assault on campus as anywhere else.

In a controversial 2014 blog post on Forbes.com titled "Drunk Female Guests Are the Gravest Threat to Fraternities," writer Bill Frezza addressed the topic of alcohol and sexual assault on campus from the viewpoint of "risk management," offering a harsh view of the "threat" that drunk women pose. The outrage in social media was immediate. While Frezza could have used a great deal more diplomacy in delivering his message, parents need to take much of what he said to heart. He cited some of the serious risks that fraternities face when holding events that offer alcohol and/or welcome inebriated guests:

- Alcohol poisoning due to overconsumption before, during, or after an event

- Death or grievous injury as a result of falling down stairs, out of a window, or off a balcony

- Death or grievous injury as a result of a pedestrian or traffic accident as guests weave their way home

What Frezza does not mention is that most college-aged students are not legally able to buy or consume alcohol—so like parents who condone high school parties with alcohol, fraternity organizations are criminally and civilly liable for the crimes that happen on their properties.

Where Frezza really stoked the ire of readers was his focus on the "false" accusations of rape that take place. Yes, there are false accusations. But it can be assumed that there are many young women and men at these parties who *are* raped. And that is something we—as parents and as a society—cannot ignore.

As a parent, you must take a serious "risk management" viewpoint of your own when sending your child to college. Without parental supervision, curfews, or boundaries, many students will engage in behavior that endangers themselves and others. This does not mean that you need to force your child to live at home forever. You can teach your child to take the same view you do—on drugs and alcohol as on other things—and to assess his or her safety and the safety of others in any situation that can occur, whether on or off campus. You can send your child off to college with a sense of empowerment, a true understanding of risk and consequences, and the ability to confidently make friends, have fun, thrive, and succeed—without overindulging.

Teenagers and college students are not dumb; they read the headlines and know the issues. They are connected to the world. Ask them in a nonjudgmental and truly curious way if they think alcohol is a concern. Ask them if they see drugs and what they think. After all, they are the ones in the trenches.

The fact is, the number one cause of sexual assault on campus may be alcohol or drug use—by either the aggressor or the victim. Drunkenness never equals consent from a man or a woman. And by making it clear that your college-aged teen should avoid situations where there is gross drunkenness and should *never* have sex with someone who is drunk, you can help empower him or her to make wise decisions.

Hazing

University organizations, for both men and women, have a long history of hazing. Awareness of the dangers of hazing has increased, and hazing practices are no longer used in many groups. But that's not to say hazing is a thing of the past—especially in college sororities and fraternities.

Hazing is one situation where male victims seldom report. Remember: Sexual assault is seldom, if ever, about sex. Many men are assaulted by members of organizations that the victims wanted to be a part of: a sports team, a fraternity, a military unit. I have worked with men who were gang-raped by fraternity "brothers" as a part of initiation; men in sports who were sodomized for poor sports performance; men who were taken advantage of by women when the men were intoxicated; straight men who were assaulted by gay men and now are tortured by questions about their sexuality; and men assaulted in the military because they did not perform according to standards or might be gay. Because of the stigma of what these men face by talking about what happened to them, often they do not report the crimes. And it's no wonder: A man who reports an assault can immediately lose every-thing—the respect of his friends, scholarships, career advancement, fraternity membership.

Fortunately, alongside rising awareness about the problems and dangers of hazing, college students can find a huge support system when they do come forward and report. In addition, plenty of worthy organizations—fraternities, sororities, and many others—do not haze. Encourage your college-aged child to explore all of the positive oppor-tunities available on campus.

Abusive Relationships

Your child may have witnessed abusive dating relationships in high school, whether the aggressor was verbally, emotionally, or physically abusive (and remember, boys and men can be victims just as girls and women can). When your child is away at school and living on or off campus in a group situation, he or she may be exposed to more of these relationships, and may see them in a brighter, uglier light.

Warn your college-aged child about these kinds of relationships, whether or not your child has witnessed them already. Make sure your teen knows how to report abuse (see chapter 8 and elsewhere about reporting specific situations) and knows how to find the local abuse shelters, which are usually in secret locations to protect the safety of victims. Give your child permission to safely and carefully help the vic-tim, call the police, and seek professional help for those involved. Warn your teen to be safe and to not get into dangerous situations. But let him or her know that doing nothing only makes the problem bigger and more dangerous for the victim and the community.

Finally, encourage your college-aged student to come to you if he or she is in an abusive situation—or, if this is difficult for some reason, to report the abuse to the police and get professional help as soon as possible.

Your College Student: The Expert on Everything

College and living away from home is not a continuation of childhood. It's time to be an adult and to learn and have fun while making adult decisions and understanding adult consequences.

An empowered, confident child has the chance to come into his or her own in the college setting. Your young adult may be adamant about how women need to take back their bodies and how men should be free to live in a world without sexual aggression. But your child needs to understand one thing: All the idealism and activism in the world will not keep him or her safe from assault if there are people out there who simply do not agree with these moral standpoints and do not care.

When my older sister came home from her first trimester of college, she suddenly thought she was the smartest eighteen-year-old on the planet. The rest of us in the house were blithering, uneducated idiots. According to her, we knew nothing of the world, and she had no problem reminding us. A few years later, I went away to college. And the same thing happened. Within a three-month period, my parents went from reasonably equipped adults . . . to utter fools. My parents rolled their eyes and continued about the process of living their lives. And like all young people and their phases, my sister and I both outgrew ours.

Talking to your college-aged child is going to be vastly different from how you have communicated with your child before. While your high schooler may have thought you were embarrassing, out of touch, controlling, or clueless, to your college student you are now uneducated and unworldly. Even the sweetest, most respectful child will embody this in one way or another. Your task is to use this to your advantage.

This may be the first time in your child's life that he or she wants to pontificate. Your child wants to talk at you and tell you things he or she thinks you don't already know. Resist the temptation to shut your child down and call him or her a mere babe in the woods. (That's what he or she is, of course, but you don't need to rub it in.) Instead, let your college student talk. Then start asking questions. Ask if he or she wants your advice. Ask permission to share your opinion. Treat young adults in the conversation as though they are the college professor they think they are. Use your questions to guide the discussion and help your college student come to wise conclusions. *Make your child think that your guidance is his or her conclusion.*

If you argue with your college student about opinions, you will only serve to solidify your child's view in his or her mind, no matter how screwed up or dangerous it is. But if you can talk to your college student in a way that makes him or her believe that your input and guidance are actually the child's idea, you will win in the long run.

Making Sure Your Child Does Not Become a Statistic

In chapter 13, I talked about how important it is to give teens real responsibility with real consequences. Internet connectivity, cars, schools, access to drugs and alcohol, and peer groups can be gateways to maturity—or they can be ingredients in a recipe for disaster. How teens handle these things gives a good indication of how they will handle life in a college atmosphere. If your child is already showing signs of problems with drugs and alcohol, allowing your child to live on a college campus is probably not the best idea, no matter how many promises your child gives you that he or she will "change" or "clean up" once away from home. An overprotected child who has had limited freedom and little ability to make healthy decisions will likely face similar struggles as he or she is barraged with a thousand bad ideas in the first week of college.

So how do you keep your son or daughter from being a statistic?

Consider an analogy from the public relations profession, a lesson followed by corporate CEOs, public figures, and other high-profile people: If you don't want what you have done to be splashed on the cover of the *New York Times*, trending in social media, or photographed and spread across the world . . . *then don't do it.* Of course, no one is perfect, and we all do things that we later regret. But if you assume that anything and everything you do can become public and embarrassing instantly—which it can—then you may think twice about certain actions.

How does this work for college students? Binge drinking, drug experimentation, sex with strangers, nude photos . . . All of these things take on a different light in the age of the Internet. Not only will photos of drunken stupors be potentially embarrassing in the short term, but they can be career-limiting once the college student tries to get an internship, apply for a job, or find a life partner. Talk to your child about sex and the repercussions, including damage to his or her reputation, STDs, the lifelong ramifications of pregnancy, and the emotional turmoil that sex in relationships can cause. No one wants to become a negative statistic—and your child doesn't have to.

Military Life

Our servicemen and servicewomen are some of the bravest, strongest, and most essential people to our nation and our safety. They stare down the barrels of guns and face dangers of all types, every single day. Sexual assault by fellow personnel should not have to be one of their concerns. But unfortunately, after some public scandals, we now know that sexual assault and cover-up in the armed forces and the military academies are more common than once thought. Men and women (in all of the branches and all of the academies) have been sexually assaulted by others of their own rank and by higher-ranking personnel. As in all cases of sexual assault, there is a huge power differential between the victim and the perpetrator. In the military, these power differentials are magnified.

When it comes to social issues, the military runs at a glacial pace. Their acumen lies in fighting wars and protecting populations, not social justice and victims' rights. Until this changes, victims of sexual assault in the military have to be extra tenacious and dedicated in reporting, because in order to seek justice, they may be risking their career.

If your son or daughter serves in or is entering the military, have an honest discussion about sexual assault in the ranks. Tell your child to do his or her best to stay safe and protected. Make it clear to your child that if anything should happen, you will be 100 percent supportive, just as you are with his or her decision to fight for our nation.

Living, Traveling, or Working Abroad

The world is a wide and wonderful place. There is no better time for global exploration than after high school, when a young adult is not encumbered by the constraints of career, family, mortgage, and the other trappings of later adulthood. But it's foolhardy to believe that the safety and protections we enjoy in the United States extend to American citizens traveling abroad. A little research and preparation can make the difference between a dream-trip-come-true and a tragedy. In fact, if your child is getting ready to live, work, or travel abroad, hand him or her this section of the book. It's a good start for anyone spending time in a new place.

Do Your Research

Encourage your child to extensively research the countries where he or she will be traveling. In the age of the Internet, with tons of information at our fingertips, this seems like a no-brainer. But you would be surprised how many college-aged kids have stepped off the plane in Mexico and wondered why no one speaks English. With a little preparation in advance, your child will be less likely to visit dangerous areas, less susceptible to crime and con artists, and safer from sexual assault.

If your child is heading abroad for a new job, make sure to check things out. Your child should not accept job offers that have not been vetted by a third party. This is a strategy of sex traffickers: They lure men and women to a foreign country with the promise of a coveted job as a model or entertainer, and then take the person's passport and force him or her into prostitution and sex trafficking. If your child is offered a job, encourage him or her to check in with the local embassy for any information that can be helpful. If your child does go, tell him or her to send the local embassy a photocopy or scan of the identification page of your child's passport.

Keep Important Documents Safe

Keep a photocopy and a scan of your child's passport in a safe place at home. If the passport is lost or stolen, or if your child is the victim of another crime, your copy can establish your child's identity, show that he or she is a citizen, and enlist the full help of authorities at the local US Embassy.

Tell your child her passport is her most prized possession and never to let anyone take it out of her possession (other than at a standard checkpoint). Your child shouldn't let anyone borrow it or say that they will "keep it safe for you." Sex traffickers have kept men and women imprisoned in foreign countries for years by simply taking the victim's passport and not allowing the victim access to law enforcement. If you can't prove you are an American and you do not have identification, it's much harder for US officials to help you.

Respect Local Laws and Customs

Your child should research the local laws and be sure not to break them. This goes for everything from hopping turnstiles to sleeping in parks to public drunkenness. You don't want your child in a foreign jail where sexual assault is rampant—or susceptible to unscrupulous police officers.

Also remind your child to research and respect the local customs. It's easy for an American woman to say, "I don't have to cover my hair, because I am an American." But in countries where such customs are required, a woman with uncovered hair may be a target for assault and rape.

In general, your child should dress as modestly as possible and try to blend in until he or she understands local norms. This applies equally to men and women. In many countries, shorts are never acceptable. In others, women may be encouraged to wear skirts that go below the knee. Walking off a train or plane in a miniskirt or shorts makes your son or daughter stick out more than they should. While in the United States we understand that women never ask for sexual assault by wearing a short skirt, we cannot expect other countries to share this understanding. Encourage your child to dress as respectfully as possible. While it sounds draconian, it can mean the difference between sexual assault and safety.

Avoid Alcohol, Drugs, and Risky Settings

Implore your child to avoid alcohol and steer clear of drugs altogether. Unless your child has lived in the area for a while and knows the locals and area customs, he or she should err on the side of caution. Drug laws vary from country to country, and even small amounts of what our society might consider "recreational" drugs can result in long jail sentences. And these sentences tend to be harder for foreigners than they are for locals with deep connections. Even in a country where drinking alcohol is permitted at a younger age, your child must use caution. Drunk people are easy targets. It's not worth it.

Also remind your child to stay out of "hinky" situations. It's easy to swagger into a dark alley at home, because he or she may have the confidence to know what is there and what is beyond. When your child visits a foreign country, encourage him or her to exercise much greater caution than at home.

Stay in Contact

Suggest that your child check in with the local embassy or consulate in every country visited. This is an easy thing to do and beneficial. The US Embassy or consulate will get your child's information so they are able to send him or her traveler alerts and be available in case of trouble. Plus, many embassies have libraries, local information in English, and other resources not found in travel guides. If your child is the victim of a sexual assault or is accused of a crime, he or she wants to be sure that one of the first calls made is to that country's US Embassy twenty-four-hour hotline.

In addition to sharing his or her whereabouts with the US authorities, your child should always let someone at home (you or a trusted friend) know his or her general location and should check in once in a while. This should make you feel better about your child's safety, and it's also a good safety measure in general.

* * *

As a parent, you are likely to have mixed feelings about sending your child off to college or into the world. This is the moment when parents realize that the actions of that child (now a young adult) in the next few years will be the culmination of all of your parenting. This may be when we parents learn whether we "did it right"—whether we did all we can to develop our child's ability to function in the real world.

Chances are, your child's success in the wider world will pleasantly surprise you.

Part Four

Your Call to Action

Chapter 15

Spreading the Word
and Reforming Our Laws

This book has dealt with a lot of scary stuff. Fortunately, you are now empowered with solid information that can help both you and your child face the world without fear—most of the time, at least. Even better, your child is becoming a hard target for predators. Your child has strong body boundaries and self-confidence. He understands how adults and children are supposed to act around one another. She knows that she never has to hug anyone she does not want to hug. Your child knows that he or she is loved and secure—and that you will always be there to listen and to offer help and a stable support system. Your child is becoming a well-armored child.

But what about the bigger picture? How can we protect other children from abuse? How can we put more child predators behind bars? How can we encourage victims of child sexual abuse, when they are ready and able, to come forward and expose what happened to them? How can we empower more victims to tell their stories and inform our communities about potential risks? How can you—as one person who is not an elected official and doesn't have "deep pockets"—be empowered to start real change in your community? Start by doing two simple things: Understand the law, and spread the word.

Understand the Law

Laws and their enforcement vary by state in the United States; in other countries, they may vary by region, province, city, or county. Do your research and find out about the laws in your area—and especially the statutes of limitation for child sex crimes. These laws can stand in the way of victims who finally dare to come forth, sometimes years or even decades later, to report abuse against them. Enacting longer statutes of limitations (or eliminating them altogether) can encourage victims to speak out—and potentially stop their abuser from harming other children. Know the statutes in your state, region, and country. Search your state's legislative website for pending legislation that is slated to extend or shorten the statutes, whether criminal or civil.

Statutes of Limitations: Criminal versus Civil

Understand the difference between criminal and civil statutes of limitations for child sexual abuse. A *criminal statute of limitation* is the amount of time that a victim has to come forward and report to the police. As a result of such a report, a district attorney or grand jury can choose to press charges and the case can go to trial, where a judge or jury can decide whether an accused predator is guilty and should go to jail. For cases of child sexual abuse, criminal statutes of limitations vary. Some states, such as Hawaii and Florida, have eliminated criminal statutes of limitations for some kinds of child sex crimes. Victims have as much time as they need to come forward to report and see justice served, unless their perpetrator dies and can no longer be sentenced to prison. Other states don't give victims much time at all. In California, there is an age limit: A victim has only until their late twenties to come forward and file charges, even if the victim believes that the perpetrator is abusing other children.

A *civil statute of limitation* is the amount of time that a victim has to come forward and file a civil lawsuit against an alleged predator or an organization that may have covered up for the alleged predator. These cases are not criminal and do not result in the perpetrator serving any kind of prison sentence. Any punishment that is rendered is usually monetary. The civil justice system and civil lawsuits serve to punish companies and individuals who engage in wrongdoing and act as a deterrent against any further wrongdoing. In other words, people are less likely to engage in bad behavior if they know they can be sued. Civil lawsuits also allow plaintiffs (the victims who are doing the suing) to get possession of documents and witnesses that can expose greater cover-up of child sex crimes. Good examples of how this works include lawsuits filed against the Catholic Church and the Boy Scouts, where victims were able to access decades' worth of documents that exposed a wide-scale cover-up of sexual abuse.

Extending or Eliminating Statutes of Limitations

Child sex abuse has long been treated as a crime of shame and secrecy. It can take victims of abuse decades to heal and be strong enough to name their abuser and face him or her in court. In addition, child sex offenders do not stop abusing, so during those decades when victims are shamed into silence, a predator can be grooming and abusing more children.

In cases of sexual abuse, the passage of time does not reduce the pain of abuse, the risk a predator poses, the distressing memories of witnesses, or the evidence of abuse. Extending the statutes of limitations allows victims to come forward and use evidence and witnesses to stop a predator in his or her tracks. Plus, if a predator knows that his or her victims may come forward even decades later, he or she may be less likely to act out on his urges. It can be a big deterrent for abusers who fear being publicly exposed and incarcerated.

Going to court—civil or criminal—is not an easy journey for victims. They must meet the burden of proof, relive horrible memories of abuse, and open themselves up to criticism, ridicule, scorn, and rejection. They have to sit through long depositions where their integrity is challenged, they must find witnesses and evidence to corroborate their story, and they must endure the long trial process. It's not a walk in the park.

But victims should never be denied the chance simply because they were too scared or damaged to come forward earlier. An even greater tragedy is when a victim of child sex crimes has no idea that he or she has rights in the courts until those rights have already expired. If you feel strongly that a child sex abuse victim has the right to face his or her abuser in court, look into your state's laws and consider whether those laws can be improved to protect all children from abuse.

Spread the Word

If legislation about the statute of limitations is pending in your state, and you are in definite support of or opposition to the bill, write your legislator and let your voice be heard. Most states also let concerned citizens provide verbal or written testimonies during hearings. The only way your legislators can know that there is a public need for a bill—or vocal support against it—is if you pick up your pen or fire up your computer and write letters. They might be some of the most important, influential letters you'll ever write.

Buy copies of this book and share them with your friends, acquaintances, and local legislators. Encourage them to spread the word among other acquaintances and lawmakers. If you live in a state with statutes of limitations that let predators get away with child sex crimes, arrange a meeting with your local representative and encourage him or her to author legislation that gives crime victims more time to come forward and accomplish justice. Because when it comes to child sex crimes, justice delayed is *not* justice denied.

For more information that you can share, the best place to start is the National Center for Victims of Crime at victimsofcrime.org. This comprehensive website is a treasure trove of resources and educational information on civil laws that protect victims and how to prevent crimes. Or contact any of the dozens of nonprofits nationwide that dedicate their entire mission or a part of their mission to extending or eliminating statutes of limitations for child sex crimes. Many of these organizations also work toward justice for all victims of crime. If you find one you like, donate your time or your money. Victims you may never meet will thank you.

Afterword

Child sexual abuse is not going away in our lifetime. That is a tragedy. It will take many generations to break the cycle, if we can even accomplish this lofty goal at all. But you and your family don't ever have to be a part of the cycle of abuse.

Now *you have the keys to creating a well-armored child*—a child who is a hard target for predators and who is empowered with the self-esteem required to repel abuse. The keys to protecting your child, no matter what age, are simple: communication, boundaries, and simple prevention tools.

The number one key to preventing child sexual abuse is to have healthy, open, and age-appropriate communication with your child. Communication means that you are able to discuss with your child what you want him or her to know . . . *and* that you listen to your child in return. Much of your child's communication will be nonverbal; your child may lack the ability, language, and maturity to tell you in words when he or she needs help, validation, support, or love. As your child gets older, communication may be cloaked by anger or frustration.

No matter how your child tries to communicate, the more you can be perceptive—and listen and react appropriately—the more your child will get the positive affirmation, guidance, love, and answers he or she needs. Your child will also be far less likely to seek affirmation from a predator.

Boundaries are often the "forgotten" tool when it comes to preventing child sexual abuse. Yet boundaries are vital—not just for safety, but also for helping our children learn and understand their bodies and abilities, and helping them feel comfortable and thrive in a sometimes scary and chaotic world. When you gently teach a child what behavior is expected from him or her, and what is a proper and right way for adults to behave, your child is far less likely to accept grooming behaviors—sexualized or "hinky" behavior from adults, or inappropriate flattery or gifts. Your child is also more likely to report abuse he or she sees, whether that abuse is by adults or other children. By reinforcing your child's strong, stable body boundaries, you are helping him or her be safer throughout life.

Finally, you now have easy-to-use prevention tools to help you arm both your own child and other children in your community. Understanding concepts like predatory grooming, reporting abuse, communication strategies, trusting your gut, and using proper language is your "ace in the hole" against predators. Comprehending the problem of child sexual abuse solves only 1 percent of the problem. But having tools at your disposal that are easy to implement seamlessly into your everyday life will help ensure that your child is anything but an easy target for sexual abuse. As your child grows and enters young adulthood, these tools will help him or her face tough decisions with maturity, common sense, and grace.

Our children are our most prized possessions. They deserve to be well-armored for life.

Acknowledgments

I am humbly grateful to my family, friends, and colleagues. Without them, this book would not exist. More specifically . . .

To Mike and Nicholas Winter and Darcy Fehringer-Mask, I love you more than words can say; to my dad, John, for his tremendous capacity to grow and for being the best friend a daughter could ever want; and to El, who loves me as if I were her own child. To Jennifer Casteix, for being the perfect Sissy, and to George Jenson, for hosting, loving, and nurturing TheWorthyAdversary.com. To my aunts Sue Peterson and Lisa Chaney, who cheer me on, laugh at my jokes, and treat my son as if he were their own.

To Jeff Anderson, who inspires me to greater successes than I ever thought possible; and to Patrick Wall, who has been my friend, cheerleader, and colleague for this entire, amazing journey.

To SNAP, the Survivors Network of those Abused by Priests, for allowing me a voice when I thought I didn't have one; to David Clohessy for being a mentor, coach, and friend; to Barb Dorris for being my partner in crime; and to Barbara Blaine for starting it all.

To Michael D'Antonio for helping me take the idea of this book and turn it into something real; to Gustavo Arellano, for tackling the hard stories and giving me and other survivors the fighting respect we have earned; and to John Manly, who taught me how to fight.

To Yvonne Kahlen and Sarah Kale for the amazing friends you are; to Jim Garcia for reading everything I have ever sent, even when it was really bad; and to Stacy Nielsen Turek, who sparked the initial idea.

To my colleagues and allies—Tim Lennon, Melanie Sakoda, Mary DeSantis, Sherida Ruiz, John Chevedden, Esther Miller, Paul Livingston, Mitch Kahle, Holly Huber, Carolyn Golojuch, the Conaty family, Elsie Boudreau, and Ken Smolka.

To Jeff Dion, Joe George, Deborah Kennedy, Katie Reed, Julie Shiroishi, and William Lobdell for your continued support of the book and my mission.

To Tyler LeBleu and his whole team at Greenleaf, especially my editors Amy McIlwaine and Marcia Meier.

And finally to Christ Lutheran School, Costa Mesa, for embracing me and giving me a platform.

About the Author

A successful writer and blogger, Joelle Casteix is also a leading national "in the trenches" expert on the prevention and exposure of childhood sexual abuse and cover-up, especially within institutions such as the Catholic Church. A former journalist, educator, and public relations professional, Joelle has taken her own experience as a victim of childhood sex crimes and devoted her career to exposing abuse, advocating on behalf of survivors, and spreading abuse prevention strategies for parents and communities.

Since 2003, Joelle has been the volunteer Western Regional Director of SNAP, the Survivors Network of those Abused by Priests. In that capacity, she has traveled the world exposing abusers; helping victims get healing, justice, and accountability; and researching predatory abuse patterns in institutions. Her expertise includes an in-depth understanding and recognition of patterns of abuse, predatory behaviors, grooming, prevention, institutional disregard, and criminal cover-up. She also conducts trainings for families, churches, and communities on how to raise empowered children and keep our communities safe from childhood sexual abuse. In addition to her work for victims, she is dedicated to the arts, sitting on the board of directors for the Follman-Young Foundation for the Arts. Joelle's other books include *The Compassionate Response: How to Help and Empower the Adult Victim of Child Sexual Abuse*, and *Yes, My Son. Wine Is One of the Five Food Groups.*

To learn more about the author, visit www.casteix.com.

Resources

This is a basic list of national referral services and support groups for victims of child sexual abuse and their family members. Many states and large cities also have expansive resources available, so a good Internet search will also help you find appropriate groups in your area.

Crisis Hotlines and Victim Advocacy

Childhelp (www.childhelp.org) runs the National Child Abuse Hotline at 1-800-4-A-CHILD. They also have a referral service that can help victims and their families gain access to thousands of therapists, care providers, support groups, and services nationwide.

Darkness to Light (www.d2l.org) offers a twenty-four-hour hotline for adult survivors of child sexual abuse, at 1-866-FOR-LIGHT. They also offer educational and crisis resources and information about legislation that helps victims.

The National Center for Victims of Crime (www.victimsofcrime.org) advocates for stronger rights and services for crime victims; provides education, training, and evaluation; and serves as a trusted source of current information on victims' issues. Their toll-free Helpline at 855-4VICTIMS assists victims who need referrals to local services across the United States.

The National Crime Victim Bar Association is the nation's first professional association of attorneys and expert witnesses dedicated to helping victims seek justice through the civil system. They provide a national attorney referral service at 844-LAW-HELP that assists survivors of crime—including child sexual abuse—in finding reputable attorneys who both understand the complexities of sex crimes against children and deal compassionately with victims and their families.

RAINN, the Rape, Abuse, and Incest National Network (www.rainn .org), offers a twenty-four-hour crisis hotline at 1-800-656-HOPE. They also offer referral and educational services, and advocacy for victims of sex crimes.

Support Groups

1in6 (www.1in6.org) helps men who have had unwanted or abusive sexual experiences in childhood live healthier, happier lives.

MaleSurvivor (www.malesurvivor.org) provides critical resources to male survivors of sexual trauma and their partners in recovery by building communities of hope, healing, and support.

SNAP, the Survivors Network of those Abused by Priests (www.snapnetwork.org) is the nation's largest support group network for men and women sexually abused in religious and institutional settings.

Survivors of Incest Anonymous (www.siawso.org) is a spiritual self-help group for child sex abuse survivors ages eighteen years or older. They are guided by a set of twelve suggested steps and twelve traditions, borrowed from AA, along with some SIA slogans and the Serenity Prayer.

Endnotes

Introduction

1 Source: https://www.ncjrs.gov/pdffiles1/ojjdp/214383.pdf

2 Source: http://www.unh.edu/ccrc/

3 Source: http://www.missingkids.com/en_US/documents/nismart
   2_nonfamily.pdf

Chapter 1

4 Source: http://www.unh.edu/ccrc/pdf/CV171.pdf

5 View the chart here: http://nsvrc.org/sites/default/files/saam_2013
   _an-overview-of-healthy-childhood-sexual-development.pdf

Chapter 5

6 Source: http://www.snapnetwork.org/links_homepage/when_priest
   _accused.htm

7. Lyon, T.D. (2002). "Scientific Support for Expert Testimony on Child Sexual Abuse Accommodation." In J.R. Conte (ed.), *Critical Issues in Child Sexual Abuse* (pp. 107–138). Newbury Park, CA: Sage, 2002.

Chapter 6

8 The article is reprinted in full at https://web.archive.org/web/20140613190102/http://christianitytoday.com/le/2014/june-online-only/my-easy-trip-from-youth-minister-to-felon.html

9 Source: https://www.psychologytoday.com/blog/spycatcher/201404/why-predators-are-attracted-careers-in-the-clergy

Chapter 7

10 Source: http://www.telegraph.co.uk/news/worldnews/northamerica/usa/11165656/John-Grisham-men-who-watch-child-porn-are-not-all-paedophiles.html

Chapter 9

11 Source: http://www.ibtimes.co.uk/child-abuse-affects-gene-responsible-stress-immunity-1458510

Index

bathroom use, teaching about, 154–55
baths, teaching privacy boundaries during, 161–63
"Battered Child Syndrome, The" (Kempe, et al.), 119
behavioral issues of preteens, 204–5
Big Brothers/Big Sisters, 242
blaming victims, 6–7, 14, 25, 52, 225
body parts and body issues
    communicating with your child about, 75–76
    early awareness of, 16
    eliminating shame about, 148
    memorizing your baby's body, 137–38
    puberty, 201, 203–4
    teaching correct names to children, 150–53
    teaching privacy boundaries, 161–63
boundaries
    about, 2, 272
    and age-appropriate freedoms for your child, 45–46
    for babies, 132–33, 136–37
    blurring by predators, 69–70
    children setting their own, 83–84
    and child's trusting relationship with parents, 16–17
    for genitalia, 153, 161
    learning in a safe environment, 26
    parent-child relationship, 45
    for preteens, 215
    for privacy, 160–64
    reinforcing, 75, 165–66
    and self-confidence of your child, 42
    and technology, 47–48, 76
Boy Scouts of America, 12, 94–95, 123
Brainstorm (Siegel), 220–21
brain vs. gut, 53–56
bruising or marks on children, 33, 138, 188–89
bullying, 10, 167, 179–80, 189, 190, 231
Buress, Hannibal, 81

C

California age limit for reporting child sexual abuse, 4, 266–67
campus sex crimes, 249, 253. See also college life

Casteix, Joelle
    abuse prevention focus, xi–xii, xiii, 3, 4, 5–6
    as high school student, 218–19
    lawsuit against teacher and school, 4
    speaking out against injustice, 93–94
    teacher's sexual abuse of, xi, 3–4, 6–7, 91, 219
Castillo, Father Alejandro, 92–93
Catholic Church
    Catholic high school, Orange County, California, 3–4, 6–7, 91, 218–19
    and convicted child sex offenders, 18, 92–93, 102
    knee-jerk defenses, 12
    priest in possession of child pornography, 102, 114–15
    Roman Catholic Diocese of Orange County, California, 4, 7
charismatic leaders, 96–99, 240, 241–43
chat rooms, 47, 192–93
Child Abuse Prevention and Treatment Act, 23–24
child as adult, 247–61
    about, 247
    living, traveling, or working abroad, 258–61
    military life, 257–58
    and sexual assault, 249–51
    talking with, 248–49
    See also college life
Childhelp National Child Abuse Hotline, x, 54, 104, 106, 128, 179, 188–89, 277
child pornography, 109–16
    about, 110–11
    bathtub pictures vs., 163
    Child Abuse Prevention and Treatment Act on, 23, 24
    minimizing pain caused to victims, 109, 113
    reporting, ix–x
    sexting, 115–16, 212–13, 233–34
    victimless crime myth, 111–16
children
    age-appropriate freedoms, 45–48
    anxiety experience, 56–57
    bruising or marks on, 33, 138, 188–89

cover-ups and secrecy (*con't.d*)
   by institutions, 95–96, 100–101
Crimes Against Children Research
   Center
criminal statues of limitations, 12–13,
   122–23, 266–68
crisis hotlines, 277–78. *See also specific*
   hotlines
customs in foreign countries, 259–60

D

Daniels, Tommy Gene, 123
Darkness to Light, 277
dating, 232–34
day care providers, 139–42
decision making by your child
   risk-taking by teenagers vs., 220–22,
     226–27
   teenagers, 231, 239
   understanding consequences, 49
denial, 7–8, 13, 48
depression, 34, 204–5
discipline and consistency, 135–37, 145
doctor or nudity games, 188
domestic abuse between parents, 43–44,
   139
drugs. *See* alcohol and drugs
"Drunk Female Guests Are the Gravest
   Threat to Fraternities" (Frezza),
   251–52

E

educating your child about sexual abuse,
   15–19. *See also* communication
   with your child
elementary school-aged children, 171–94
   about, 171–72, 193–94
   abuse and bullying in school, 179–80,
     189
   child-on-child abuse, 189–91
   encouraging tattletales, 190–91
   gossip mills/rumors, 180
   helicopter parents, 180
   and Internet use, 191–93
   no closed doors policy, 186
   "observing glasses" of parents,
     177–78
   parental responses to problems,
     174–75, 179

   partnering with your child's teacher,
     178–79
   peer group red-flag behaviors,
     187–89
   peer groups, 182–86
   responsibilities of, 172–74
   school cover-up as unacceptable,
     181–82
   sex discussions among children,
     184–85
   sex education, 182
   sleepovers, 183–84
   talking with your child about school,
     176–77
   transparency of school decisions, 181
emotions
   of preteens, 196, 197–98, 207–8
   response to accusations of abuse by
     others, 85–87
   of teenagers, 218
   of victims of child sexual abuse, 105
employment in foreign countries, 259
employment of teenagers, 234–36
engaged parents, 39
Enron, 94

F

families
   about, 104–5
   blaming victims, 25
   building family bonds, 214
   family members as predators, 83–84
   incest and incest victims, 73, 83–84,
     105–7
fear, plague of, 40–41, 79
federal punishment for child
   pornography, 110
feelings, 57–59 *See also* gut feelings
female predators. *See* women as predators
fighting back, 31–32
Finn, Bishop Robert, 102, 114–15
flirting by teenagers with adults, 26–27
foreign travel, 239–40, 250, 258–61
freedoms
   age-appropriate, 45–48
   of elementary school-aged children,
     171, 180
   of preteens, 205, 207
   of teenagers, 230, 232
   of toddlers, 160

girls abused by adult women, 30, 83
gut instincts ignored, 52, 227–28
historic blaming and shaming of
    victim, 6–7, 14, 148, 225
home situation before, during, and
    after abuse, 38–39
incest, 73, 83–84, 105–7
lawsuits filed by, 4, 102–3, 268
and legal process, 28
love for abuser, 64, 69–70, 71, 73, 84,
    207–8
mental state before and after abuse,
    12–13, 15
minimizing a class of, 25
need to process what happened to
    them, 27–28
and news media, 9–10, 122
reporting abuse, 8
shame of preteen victims, 205–6
value of getting proof, 4–5
See also grooming
volunteering in your child's classroom,
    178–79
vulnerability of children
    about, 2–3, 5, 29–30
    behavioral issue related, 204–5
    and bullying, 10, 179
    and child pornography, 112
    and fearfulness of child, 41
    and female predators, 30, 83
    grooming examples, 65–67, 68–69

from lack of self-confidence, 42
preteens, 197–98
reasons for, 38–39, 44
self-esteem as protection from, 200
from stress and chaos as an infant, 139

W

wartime mass rapes, 32
whistleblowers, treatment of, 104
"Why Predators Are Attracted to Careers
    in the Clergy" (Navarro), 98
women as predators
    about, 11–12, 82, 83
    and boys, 18, 30, 82–83, 203
    and children in puberty, 198
    and girls, 30, 83
    Letourneau, Mary Kay, 13, 82–83, 201
Worthy Adversary, The (blog), 166–67, 273